WRITING

A SOURCEBOOK OF EXERCISES AND ASSIGNMENTS

Deborah Gunther • Lynda Marin

Joan Maxwell • Jeri Weiss

 ADDISON-WESLEY PUBLISHING COMPANY

Menlo Park, California • Reading, Massachusetts
London • Amsterdam • Don Mills, Ontario • Sydney

ACKNOWLEDGEMENTS

The authors are grateful to Billie Frederick and Peter Drewniany of the English Department of Pennsylvania's Harrisburg Academy for their help in classroom-testing these exercises and for their many cogent suggestions.

We were given much useful advice and encouragement by Nancy Masland, Director of Green Fields School in Tucson, Arizona; David Maxwell; Kenneth Millar; Andrew D. Sinauer; and Jack Taylor.

Inspiration for certain exercises came from Christina Adam of the Oakwood School, North Hollywood, California; Louis Dexter, M.D., of Boston's Peter Bent Brigham Hospital; and Priscilla Oakes of California State University at Fullerton.

We benefitted enormously from the penetrating criticisms of the dozen or more writing teachers at high schools and colleges around the United States who have reviewed this work in manuscript. We regret that, because their reviews were anonymous, we are unable to thank them here by name.

We deeply appreciate Charles Schultz's permission to reprint his endearing biography of Snoopy.

We are indebted to Hasel Popjak for her meticulous and knowledgeable proofreading.

Ruth Gluck's skill at deciphering our scribblings, her keen eye for discrepancies, redundancies, and opacities, and her great patience with the four of us were and remain invaluable.

Our greatest debt is to our students, past and present, who made this book possible.

This book is in the ADDISON-WESLEY INNOVATIVE SERIES.

ISBN 0-201-02632-5
DEFGHIJK-AL-8987654

ABOUT THE AUTHORS

Deborah Gunther has had fourteen years' experience teaching writing at the high school and junior high school levels. She has taught at inner city public schools and in suburban private schools. She received her BA and secondary school teaching credential from the University of Califor-nia at Berkeley.

Lynda Marin received her MA in English from the University of California at Los Angeles. Her ten years of teaching writing include work at the university, high school, and junior high school levels. She is currently head of a Middle School in Los Angeles.

Joan Maxwell, a former textbook editor at Harper & Row Publishers, has taught writing for five years at the high school level. A graduate of Bryn Mawr College, she is currently a professional writer and heads her own writing service in Los Angeles.

Jeri Weiss received her PhD in English from the University of California at Los Angeles. Her fifteen years' experience teaching writing include work at the high school, community college, and university levels. She is currently Dean of Students and head of the writing program at an independent secondary school in Los Angeles.

ABOUT GENDER

This is a book about writing well. In our opinion good writing is simple and clear. We find it impossible to write simply and clearly while using the very awkward constructions of "he or she", "him or her", and "his or her". Since the accepted generic singular personal pronouns in the English language are he, his, and him, we have consciously chosen to employ them in the interest of clarity of style.

We chose to emphasize clarity above all other considerations because the effectiveness of this book as a tool to help teachers teach writing would otherwise be seriously impaired. We wish to point out that the publishing guidelines for the equal treatment of the sexes (drawn up by McGraw-Hill and currently in general use by the publishing industry) allow for this choice in the interest of clarity.

As four women who know that the sexes are equal, we ask that you not take our use of the masculine pronoun as a political or philosophical statement.

CONTENTS

---

1. Level.
2. Class periods required.

4   EXPOSITION, ANALYSIS, AND ARGUMENT

5   MOTIVATORS

APPENDICES

WHY THIS BOOK

Behind this book is a history which we suspect may sound familiar to you. When we first started teaching writing, we turned to our own educations to provide us with models for our teaching. We used grammar books to give rules and explain how language works. We used rhetoric books to provide theories about style, organization, and usage. We used composition books to prescribe formulas for practicing and improving writing and to furnish illustrative examples.

Those of our students who shared our predilection for language readily applied these rules, theories, and formulas to their writing. The majority of our students, however, when confronted with a blank piece of paper and an essay assignment, simply could not connect the rules, theories, and formulas to their own writing process. It made no difference where we taught: in poverty area junior highs, in suburban private high schools, in urban junior colleges, or in large universities; it made no difference whom we taught: children or adults, educationally handicapped or National Merit Scholars. We still found that many of our students were not able to apply our rules, theories, and formulas to their own writing.

When we began to share our frustrations about teaching writing, we found many other writing teachers with similar feelings. It was at this time, the late '60s, that the professional journals began to voice our dilemma. Indeed, several books appeared about an alternative, experiential approach to teaching writing. Some of these diagnosed the problems with which we were struggling, while others offered suggestions for assignments and activities which were intended to move students from their life experience into the writing experience. The new books helped us engage students in the act of writing, but they did not articulate a way for us to help students connect their experience of life with the skill of writing. Our students' new enthusiasm pleased us, but their impoverished skills continued to nag at us.

Integrating Experience with Writing Practice, Skill, and Theory

In the early '70s, each of us, alone and together, developed a number of exercises and activities to enable students to integrate personal experience, writing practice, technical skill, and theory. The exercises and activities were not in themselves unique; all earnest teachers of writing have created such exercises. What was unique about them was their careful and deliberate structuring to enable students to consistently experience the connection between what they were trying to say and the skills they needed to say it effectively.

Over the past three years, the four of us have worked together to collect, combine, refine, and test these exercises. This book is the result of our efforts.

Step by Step Through A Complete Writing Experience

In all the books we have seen, including those which focus on the experiential approach, each writing exercise has been sketched in a brief paragraph. The actual process the teacher and students needed to go through to turn it into a fruitful writing experience was neglected. By contrast, each exercise and activity in this book helps the teacher take the student, step by step, through a complete writing experience. The classroom activity, discussion, student writing, and subsequent analysis have been first broken down into their component parts and then put into the sequence that our classroom testing has shown us is most effective.

Students' Writing as Models

At the heart of the exercises in this book are three assumptions we feel the need to explain. The first has to do with the use of exemplary prose models as teaching aids. To help us shape a classroom writing experience, we occasionally show students written models before we ask them to write, but not very often. Usually, after they have completed an exercise, we use the students' own writing as models to illustrate the skills and theories we want them to learn. In "First Day Back," page 3, for instance, without labeling the writing skills involved, we ask each student to try writing about an object, using four specific approaches. Later, in classroom discussion, the student analyzes his own paper to begin to identify which techniques of objective, subjective, associative, and imaginative writing he already knows, and which ones he still needs to learn.

The models students produce themselves are often more useful to them than the polished prose of masters which teachers have traditionally provided, but which seems to intimidate more than enlighten.

When we have our students begin writing without models, relying instead on structured writing, we avoid asking them to compete with masters of the craft in a contest from which they can only hope to emerge a shadowy second. Freed from this unequal competition, students are more likely to accept the challenge of writing activities wholeheartedly.

Students Share Their Work

A second assumption upon which the exercises in this book are based has to do with the positive value of students sharing their work with one another. Most of us, along with our students, find the process of sharing student writing in the classroom difficult at first. Students initially resist sharing their papers: they are insecure about their writing abilities; they are afraid of judgment and ridicule; they secretly believe their papers are expected to be perfect; and they openly disbelieve that their classmates are capable of offering constructive criticism. We, too, in the beginning, resisted having students share their own papers because we wanted to protect their feelings from group exposure and ourselves from possibly having to mediate in an uncontrollably critical atmosphere. Indeed, we believed that we were the only ones capable of perceptive, responsible criticism in the classroom.

We have moved from that position because we have found that, however much students initially resist sharing their work with the group, this resistance is worth overcoming. When students share their own papers and respond to others' papers, they gain a confidence which no one teacher alone can give them. When students have a framework in which to locate problems and solutions for one another's writing, they gain the very critical skills which they dearly need in order to improve their own writing. And when students provide an audience for one another, they gain immediate feedback about the impact and effectiveness of their writing techniques. This emphasis on group sharing and improvement of skills helps to create a workshop atmosphere in the classroom, giving each student the opportunity to use the group to help him further refine his work.

A Workshop Atmosphere

A third assumption on which this book rests, closely connected to the second one, has to do with the teacher's role in establishing a workshop atmosphere. We have found this role demanding, challenging, and, in the end, deeply satisfying. It requires us to relinquish our image of ourselves as a cornucopia of wisdom and, instead, to direct our energies toward showing our students how to do for themselves much of what we earlier assumed only we could do for them. This role requires us to be facilitators, helping students shape their activities and discussions so that they provide one another with constructive criticism and support. In this way we enable students to gain self-confidence from one another rather than just from their interactions with us. We have found that directing our energies in this manner allows us to approach our students' needs more effectively and realistically regardless of class size. Finally, our fulfillment comes from shaping a responsive classroom community where, in the process of teaching writing skills, we have helped students experience a broader competence and independence as well.

HOW TO USE THIS BOOK

We have tried to design this book so that it will be useful to anyone teaching writing at the high school level, the junior high school level, or the remedial level in college. We have included 54 exercises, far more than a year's work, so you will have a wide variety from which to choose. Some assignments can be used individually, while others are part of longer sequences. All can be adapted to your own curriculum. Use the annotated Table of Contents on page iv, check the Index of Exercises by Writing Skill on page 217, and thumb through the exercises themselves to find what you need.

Each exercise follows the same order of presentation. At the top we give its PURPOSE AND DESCRIPTION — enough for you to decide whether or not it might be useful. Then we characterize it by approximate LEVEL of difficulty for the student, so you can decide whether or not it would be appropriate for your class. We specify under CLASS PERIODS the approximate amount of class time required to complete the exercise. And we describe under ADVANCE PREPARATION exactly what must be done by the teacher before the first class meeting. (If you have seen your preparation time suddenly vanish, you may be interested to learn that there are 20 exercises here which require no advance preparation.) Next comes a detailed description of the ACTIVITY, with each step of the classroom exercise and associated homework listed sequentially. Finally, under SPECIAL POINTS, we describe what we have learned from using this exercise in our own classes—each one has been classroom tested—and offer what we feel are useful hints on its presentation.

In some exercises we have asked you to duplicate a passage and hand it out to the students. These HANDOUTS are so marked. To facilitate their duplication, the publisher has made them available in an 8½ by 11 inch format as a separate publication.

It may seem at times that we have stated the obvious in our step-by-step delineation of every exercise. We have done so knowingly, in an attempt to render each exercise fully accountable for what it purports to do. As a part of this process, virtually every exercise contains examples of one kind or another. These examples are enclosed in brackets.

We urge the novice teacher to follow the instructions for the exercises quite closely. Every detail has been tried out in the classroom, and we know each works. We hope the more experienced teacher will find some new ideas here, as well as new ways to use familiar exercises.

The exercises in this book can be used in conjunction with grammar and rhetoric books to create a complete writing course for your students. You may use them as part of a prescribed writing curriculum, or as part of your own course outline. You may find the six course outlines which appear in the Appendix (page 209) of some use as you plan your own course. The outlines are for both semester and year courses, and are structured for beginning, intermediate, and advanced students.

We invite you to consult this book as you would another writing teacher for ideas and suggestions, and use them as you will.

ON COPING WITH LARGE NUMBERS
OF STUDENT PAPERS

We know the only way students can learn how to write is by writing; but we also know that when we give a writing assignment, we invariably end up with a large mound of papers to be corrected. If we have five sections of 40 students each, the mounds of papers needing correction mount up rapidly.

Although we believe that our students must learn how to write and that they can do so only by writing, nearly all of us have too many students to permit us to devote the kind of detailed personal attention we would like to give to each student's every paper. We have learned that we must compromise, not in the length or frequency of writing assignments, but in the ways in which we help our students evaluate their progress. Here are several techniques which help us cope when papers start piling up.

Correct Only Some of the Finished Papers in Depth.

Pick an important technique or two in which your students need practice [logic, sentence structure, paragraphing] and concentrate your energies there. When you assign a writing exercise, you can tell the students what skill you intend to focus on in your corrections, thus affording them the opportunity to concentrate specifically on it as they write. Or, you can wait until the papers are completed to announce the skill you will focus on, thus preventing students from trying to avoid work by, for example, writing superb sentences but ignoring spelling. Either way, you will be able to cover all important skills more than once during a semester.

Correct Only Some of the Finished Papers.

Give a series of writing assignments and require that all students hand in completed papers for all assignments. Then permit students to specify which 1 out of 3 (or 2 out of 4) they wish to have corrected in depth. You will probably want to skim all the papers to make sure the students did the necessary work, but you will have to spend a significant amount of time on only a portion of the papers.

Require Legibility.

It took us years to come up with the courage to make this mandatory, but we now do so. Hard-to-read papers take much longer to correct, are almost impossible to read out loud, and obscure whatever intellectual virtues they may possess. Consequently, we are absolutely inflexible on this subject. Students rail at being asked to type or print neatly, but they give in if they have to. An important side benefit of requiring legibility is the possibility that students will do at least some editing while preparing final copy.

Read and Discuss Papers in Class.

A great deal of work can be done by reading papers out loud and by encouraging thoughtful class discussion in a workshop atmosphere. When a student's paper has been read to the class, you do not have to repeat in writing the points made in class discussion.

Create a Constructive Atmosphere.

The first time a paper is read to the class as a whole, concentrate on setting a positive tone throughout the subsequent discussion. Be careful to direct all remarks toward improving the paper in order to make the group analysis useful to the author and to prevent other class members from indulging in personal attack. Maintain this supportive tone whenever a paper is read.

Allow Students Privacy.

Some students are uneasy about public examination of their work. We therefore permit them to stipulate "Not To Be Read Out Loud" at the top of any paper, but monitor the frequency of such stipulations carefully. If a student invariably refuses to let his paper be read, we attempt to resolve the problem in a private discussion.

Read Finished Papers to the Entire Class.

You can read all the papers out loud yourself, thus affording anonymity to authors and an equally even verbal presentation of each paper. You can ask students to read their own work, providing them with useful practice at reading out loud. With advanced classes only, you can pass the papers out to random readers so the author can hear how his paper sounds and the reader can practice public speaking. Readers should first read others' papers silently to make sure they understand the word flow and to check any questions with the authors. A poor writer would find this a humiliating experience because all of his flaws would be made glaringly apparent by an amateur reading. This approach should be avoided with beginning and even intermediate classes.

Focus Students' Attention.

Before a paper is read out loud, assign individual students or small groups particular features to listen for. You can ask one group to pay attention to logic, one to grammar, one to tone, and so on. If students do not have something specific to consider when they are listening to a paper, their responses to it are often general and vague. By asking students to pay close attention to specific areas, you limit but focus their awareness. When we use this technique, we are careful to vary the groups' assigned areas of concentration to provide each student with practice in all areas of editorial analysis.

Divide the Class into Smaller Groups.

A variation on in-class reading is to set up two or more separate groups in different corners of the classroom and have students read their papers to their respective groups. You can move from group to group to keep things going smoothly. While this allows more students to read their papers during a class period, it has certain obvious limitations. Students have to be cooperative and sufficiently adept at analysis to be able to make useful comments to one another without your full-time supervision. Nonetheless, this can be a useful approach with certain classes.

Ask Students to Edit Another's Work.

If the atmosphere in the class is positive and if the students have become fairly skilled at analyzing and editing through the process of group analysis, you can have students work in pairs—exchanging papers from time to time and criticizing one another's work. The editing can be done in class or as homework. If you and the students prefer, the results can be kept private between the two students. Alternatively, student editors can be asked to present their partner's paper and their editorial comments to the class as a whole. This approach involves the author and the editor together and can be a useful teaching tool, as it permits you to discuss both the original paper and the analysis.

Discuss Work in Progress.

We have found that if we encourage students to discuss with the class any difficulties they encounter while in the process of writing an assignment, other students profit from the discussion and we are saved a lot of repetitive comments on the final product. To this end, we often encourage students to read excerpts from their assignments which are not yet in final form.

One particularly pleasant aspect of discussing work in progress is that the emphasis is entirely on improvement. The usefulness of class discussion becomes obvious to students because they can immediately revise their papers to take advantage of what they have learned, free of the weight of corrective marks and grades. Insecure students benefit particularly from this process.

We also endeavor to talk about work in progress with students, both as a group and individually, when they are in the process of writing an exercise in the classroom.

Schedule Individual Conferences.

If your schedule permits, see students periodically in individual conferences about their work. This is often a most useful experience for them, and also allows you to discuss particular problems which might otherwise require lengthy written comments.

A creative mix of these techniques will permit even large numbers of students to benefit from extensive and varied analyses of their papers—and the pleasure you get from teaching writing will be increased as well.

1 OBSERVATION, DESCRIPTION, AND NARRATION

We begin this section with a classroom exercise called First Day Back, followed by a game which clarifies the differences between abstract and concrete description. We then include seven exercises which ask students to observe each other; strangers, or new places, and then select appropriate detail to write descriptive essays based on their observations.

We also include five exercises which sharpen descriptive techniques. Some ask students to use the five senses or to choose words which paint vivid pictures with sensual detail; others emphasize precise word choice in describing objects or describing a process.

FIRST DAY BACK

PURPOSE AND DESCRIPTION

A good initial exercise to help students and teachers determine students' writing strengths and weaknesses. Each student writes about an object from four different approaches: objective, subjective, associative, and imaginative. This exercise helps the student and teacher determine which approaches need development for improved writing.

LEVEL   Any.

CLASS PERIODS   Two.

ADVANCE PREPARATION

Bring a number of objects to class which students can identify but with which they are not too familiar, perhaps things they might have known as young children or things they would not normally see in school [a bird's nest, a cactus skeleton, a seashell, a piggy bank]. Put all the objects in a box large enough to keep them from being piled on top of each other. Bring a few more objects than there are people in the class. Bring this box to class for both days of the exercise.

ACTIVITY   Day One

Hold the box just above eye level of each student and ask him to reach in carefully and take out the first item he touches. If your class is large, your time short, or the objects fragile, you might randomly reach into the box yourself to give each student an item. When everybody has selected an object, ask each student to write a description of the object he has chosen. If the students ask what you mean by "description," tell them to use as many of their five senses as possible to help them describe the object. Do not elaborate further on directions. Allow 5–7 minutes for these descriptions.

Second, ask students to respond to their objects by describing how they feel toward the objects. Again, do not elaborate on directions. Allow the same amount of time for this phase of the exercise.

Third, ask them to free associate—using their objects as a jumping

3

off point. You can help them start by saying, "Look at your object. Write the first word that comes to your mind and then simply keep writing. The only rule is *not* to stop writing. If nothing comes to mind write "nothing" repeatedly until some other words or phrases come to you. Don't worry about making sense." (This may be a difficult process for some students because they are so used to being asked for structured grammatical expression.) Make sure you keep the time for this free association consistent with the previous time limit.

Fourth, ask students to write a short fantasy about their objects. To get them started you might ask them, "What's the strangest thing that could happen to this object?" or, "What is an adventure it could have experienced?" Give the students the same amount of time for this last phase of the exercise.

Finally, ask students to note in the margin which parts they enjoyed writing and which they found difficult. Ask them also to mark the part for which they think they were allotted the most time.

This part of the exercise will take up an entire class period. At this point, collect the papers and objects.

Day Two

Pass out the papers, unmarked. (The absence of red corrections is always a pleasant surprise.) First, discuss with the whole class what a physical description consists of: size, shape, weight, material, texture, colors. Ask the students to note in the margins of their papers any of these basic elements of description they missed. Have the objects available in the room in case students need to refer to them.

Second, define together a subjective response. Talk about the difference between "It's nice" and "I like it." Point out that the first statement talks about the object but leaves the first person pronoun entirely out of the picture. Subjective responses, stated directly, come from people and express feelings.

Third, ask the students to share how they experienced free association. Did they write continuously, need to stop and think, cross things out, tend towards categories of words [all verbs, or all families—names of animals for instance], tend towards phrases, lapse into lengthy prose, avoid definable patterns? Speculate about the value of free association. How is it a tool for more structured writing? How can it help students

4

identify their personal methods of storing information? How can the language of association lend life and individuality to structured ideas?

Lastly, ask some of the students to share their fantasy section with the class and to look at the way their attitudes, stated or implied in previous sections, shaped their fantasies. How did the subjective response relate to the fantasy? If a student hated his object, did he alter the object in the fantasy to make it more likeable, or did he have something very negative happen to it? Help students see that their imaginations can often help them identify attitudes and that point of view can sometimes be located through fantasy.

Be sure to point out that the same amount of time was allotted to each phase of this exercise. Students will often think that they were allotted less time for the part of the exercise for which they did the most writing.

SPECIAL POINTS

We use this exercise at the beginning of the semester because we want to encourage individuality and self-evaluation on the part of the students. This exercise directs students to appeal to their own senses, their own feelings, their own associations, and their own imaginations. To do this most effectively, it is essential that each student work individually with an object. In this way each student has his own starting point and is not encouraged to compete with anyone else. In the same spirit each student must focus only on his own work during the follow-up discussion.

While the exercise is in progress during the first day, if class size permits watch the students and take brief notes on their behavior. Which parts of the exercise seem especially easy or difficult for each student? During the free association, for example, note the students who write consistently and those who stop and think in between each word and phrase. Do some students use only the first few minutes to write and then put down their pens—positive that they've said all they could think of? Observe attitudes that come out during the follow-up discussion about the various parts of the exercise. Some students may resist one approach, or be stumped by another, and be engaged by yet another. The more observations you can make, the easier it will be to help students determine which approaches need development.

After you have collected the papers, compare your observations with the students' writing. Do not put any marks or corrections on the students' papers, but you may want to make brief notes for yourself on a separate paper—specifying the areas in which students were most and least competent.

1. How well could a student distinguish between the four approaches?

2. To what extent was a student able to use his senses in the descriptive section?

3. How many students started the subjective response with "I think," or "My object is . . ."?

4. Which students were not able to write in an uninterrupted flow of words and phrases during the free association?

5. Was a student able to express an attitude about the object or about some related idea through the fantasy?

The second day's discussion requires each student to determine for himself which were his strongest and weakest sections. When students evaluate their own writing strengths and weaknesses, those evaluations often have some positive influence on subsequent writing. This exercise is also an excellent springboard for the first student-teacher conference when you may want to corroborate or modify the student's self-evaluation based on your own observations.

THE ABSTRACTION GAME

PURPOSE AND DESCRIPTION

An effective introduction to descriptive writing. A group exercise to explore varying levels of description from the most concrete to the highly metaphorical. A blindfolded student attempts to identify an object using descriptions supplied by the class.

LEVEL   Any.

CLASS PERIODS   One.

ADVANCE PREPARATION

Bring to class a half dozen familiar objects [a tube of lipstick, a spark plug, a book of matches, a hand–operated can opener, an eyelash curler, a road flare].

ACTIVITY

Discuss with the class the concept of levels of abstraction. Start by writing on the chalkboard a highly abstract word such as "animal." Then ask the students to provide progressively more concrete and narrow words derived from that abstract word, and write each of these on the board in a list. For example: animal, cow, milk cow, spotted milk cow, Holstein, Farmer Brown's Holstein, Farmer Brown's prize Holstein, Farmer Brown's prize Holstein Bessie.

Now discuss the relationship between levels of abstraction and good description. Point out that good description uses a range of concrete to general words and must include more than one level of abstraction to be accurate and vivid. Neither "Bessie" nor "animal" is a satisfactory description on its own.

Next, tell the students that they are going to play a game to practice using these various levels of abstraction in description and to see how each level helps to create effective description. Explain the rules of the game. A volunteer is blindfolded and seated in front of the class. The class then passes from person to person one of the objects you brought. As each student holds the object, he gives one descriptive detail to the blindfolded volunteer. Each detail must belong to a specific level of abstraction named beforehand by the teacher. The teacher will specify three different levels and assign one third of the students to each level. For example, in a class of thirty students, ten students would give a concrete detail; the next ten would give a more abstract detail; the final ten would offer highly abstract details. The blindfolded student attempts to guess what the object is whenever he feels he has enough information to guess intelligently.

Have the class begin the descriptions at the most concrete level with sensory information such as color, weight, size, texture, taste, smell, shape. [Using the spark plug, the following hints might be provided by successive students: "It is metal." "It is also ceramic." "The ceramic is whitish." "I can hide it in my fist." "It is heavy for its size."]

After ten students have contributed at this level, instruct the next ten students to supply broader, more abstract information, such as an environment or a function of the object. [This object is discolored and darkened by use." "This object provides necessary impetus for an engine." "I wouldn't want to touch it while it was working." "There are often five others like it in its company."]

Finally, ten more students provide even more highly abstract information which includes comparison or metaphor. ["A spurt of lightning comes from one end." "It looks like a miniature rocket ship."]

If the blindfolded student cannot guess the identity of the object by the end of the third round, ask the class to return to the first level of description and repeat the descriptive process—supplying new details for the same object.

Each time a student guesses the mystery object, discuss with him and with the class which particular clue helped him to guess and why it enabled him to fit together the previously supplied information.

With a second object, and a second blindfolded volunteer, instruct the class to play the same game again. But this time ask the students to work from the most abstract metaphorical level of description down to the most concrete level.

Be sure to try both methods of playing the game so that the class will see that, in order to correctly identify the object, the blindfolded students need both abstract and concrete description. The volunteers will generally be able to guess the object only during the third round of description, no matter at which level the game was begun. Information which is limited either to the concrete or to the abstract is usually not sufficient to enable the volunteer to guess successfully.

For homework ask each student to write an essay describing a familiar object. The identity of the object should not be kept secret in the essay. The point of the essay is to describe the object fully, using language from the concrete to the highly abstract level. Possible objects to describe are a vegetable, a piece of fruit, a kitchen utensil, a piece of hardware, an automobile, a small electrical appliance.

SPECIAL POINTS

We have found this game to be a good beginning activity in teaching descriptive writing. Those students who tend to be vague will see the need for concrete detail to anchor their description. Those who write concretely, but without much imagination, will see the effectiveness of broadening and enlivening their descriptions with metaphor and comparison. The game is also a good vehicle for pointing out the difference between telling detail and extraneous detail. It is easy to see which descriptions help a student to guess an object and which ones add nothing new or illuminating to the guesswork of the blindfolded volunteer.

For the first couple of rounds you may wish to have someone record on the chalkboard the clues provided; then use that information in the discussion following each part of the game. In this way, you can trace the progressively more abstract or concrete nature of the description.

STUDENT BIOGRAPHIES

PURPOSE AND DESCRIPTION

To help students learn how to integrate information, observations, and impressions. Students write biographical sketches of each other based on personal interviews.

LEVEL   Beginning and intermediate.

CLASS PERIODS   Four.

ADVANCE PREPARATION

Duplicate the handout for "The Interview," page 150, to accompany this exercise.

ACTIVITY   Day One

Pass out the handout on Interviews and have students read it to themselves. Ask the students to supply further examples of directive and non-directive questions. Write some of these on the chalkboard. Then, to give students practice in interviewing, become yourself the subject of a class interview. Have the students direct questions to you. Tell them to pursue, with questions, some specific points of information you allude to with your initial general responses. If you are uncomfortable about answering personal questions from the class, you may want to become an imaginary character to participate in this interview.

When the students have practiced being non-directive and pursuing specific information, ask them to look around the room and pick out the two people they know least well. Now ask them to arrange themselves in pairs with one of those least known people. If this arrangement doesn't work perfectly, at least make sure that students are not paired up with their closest friends.

Tell the pairs that each partner will have almost an entire class period to interview the other for the purpose of writing a biographical sketch, a short account of who a person is and how he lives. Before the interviews begin, give each student a few minutes to write down a list of questions he would particularly like to ask his partner. Students may not want to stick to these lists, but they are good to fall back on if an interview lapses into silence. Emphasize to the students that the more sincerely interested they become in the person they are interviewing, the more interesting their sketches will be. Point out that if they pursue specific information about their subjects they will be able to write a more substantial and colorful biography.

Have the partners of each pair decide which of them will be the first interviewer; then allow them to begin. Tell interviewers to have a pencil and paper ready to take notes. Note how much time they have until class ends. Tell the students they will have 35-40 minutes for each interview and that the interview will continue the next day until they have used up the full time allotted. Make sure that each interview gets equal time and that all interviews take place in the quiet, supervised atmosphere of the classroom. If you see that any pair of students is having difficulty with the interviewing process, step in and ask a leading question accompanied by a few follow-up questions to get them started.

A few minutes before the class is over, stop the interviews and give the interviewers a chance to write down any questions the first part of the interview may have led them to want to ask the next day. Tell those students just interviewed that, based on their experience, they may want to modify or add to their own list of questions to be used when they are interviewers.

Day Two

Have the pairs meet again to finish the first interview. When the time is up, have the pairs exchange roles so that the student previously interviewed becomes the interviewer. With planning, the entire interviewing process can be finished by the end of the second day. At that time ask the students to bring their notes to class for the next day's activity.

Day Three

Tell the students that they are now going to use the information they gained during the interviews to write a biographical sketch of their partner (of at least three paragraphs). Be sure the students understand that each one needs to decide on some organizing principle based on his particular information. Discuss briefly how they might select such a

11

principle. Did the subject talk a lot about school work, vacations, a special interest, frustrations, or family? If no one aspect of his life was stressed, might the interviewer's observations of the subject provide a framework? For example, did the subject seem relaxed, nervous, impatient, removed, or energetic? What physical gestures or expressions communicated information beyond what was actually said?

Point out that the biographers must rely on their own perceptions of their partners during the interview and that their own interpretations, based on observation, will lend personality and point of view to their sketches.

After the students have determined their organizing principles, have them begin their sketches in class and tell them to complete the sketches for homework. At this point, some students may need to return to their subjects to get additional detail to support their organizing principles.

Day Four

Have partners exchange the finished sketches and check the accuracy of factual information. Then have students share these sketches with the class. Ask the listening students to identify the organizing principle the writer used. Ask them to comment on which parts of the sketch particularly interested them, which details stood out in their minds, and what they wanted to know more about. Either before or after discussing the biographical sketches, students will probably want to comment on the experience of interviewing and being interviewed. Since all of the students have experienced both sides of the interview process, they usually have specific information to contribute to this discussion.

SPECIAL POINTS

We have found that this exercise helps classes to establish a more personal communicative atmosphere. In order for this to happen, students must participate sincerely in the interviews. Students who feel hostility toward each other will not be able to have good interviews. Watch for pairs which are not working well together so that you may help set a tone and direction for their interviews by providing them with a few provocative questions. Occasionally certain pairs need to be rearranged. This happens infrequently, however, because the students usually choose partners with whom they would like to work.

This exercise helps students learn to evaluate the quality and quantity of their material, and to establish a point of view. Because the interviews require students to decide for themselves what is meaningful and interesting to know about another person and what is not, biographies which simply list the members of a family or the hobbies of the subject are rare. Furthermore, most students find, when it comes to actually writing the biographies, that they have to leave out certain information because it doesn't develop the main points they have chosen to make. They also often find, when they come to the writing process, that they want to know much more than they asked for during the interview. These kinds of realizations, made on their own, leave lasting impressions which, in turn, help students improve their techniques in later assignments that require the gathering and organizing of information.

To help students organize their essays, you may wish to distribute the handout on outlines, page 183.

ELEMENTARY, MY DEAR WATSON

PURPOSE AND DESCRIPTION

To promote careful observation. Students find and follow a stranger in a public place, attempt to learn as much as they can about the stranger, and then write an essay about their conclusions.

LEVEL   Any.

CLASS PERIODS   Two half-periods.

ADVANCE PREPARATION

Bring a copy of this description to class from Arthur Conan Doyle's "The Red Headed League". It shows the great detective Sherlock Holmes telling his friend Watson about Mr. Jabez Wilson, a new client who has just arrived at the Holmes residence:

> 'Beyond the obvious facts that he has at some time done manual labour, that he takes snuff, that he is a Freemason, that he has been in China, and that he has done a considerable amount of writing lately, I can deduce nothing else.'
>
> Mr. Jabez Wilson started up in his chair, with his forefinger upon the paper, but his eyes upon my companion.
>
> 'How in the name of good fortune, did you know all that, Mr. Holmes?' he asked. 'How did you know, for example, that I did manual labour? It's as true as gospel, for I began as a ship's carpenter.'
>
> 'Your hands, my dear sir. Your right hand is quite a size larger than your left. You have worked with it, and the muscles are more developed.'
>
> 'Well, the snuff, then, and the Freemasonry?'
>
> 'I won't insult your intelligence by telling you how I read that, especially as, rather against the strict rules of your order, you use an arc-and-compass breastpin.'
>
> 'Ah, of course, I forgot that. But the writing?'
>
> 'What else can be indicated by that right cuff so very shiny for five inches, and the left one with the smooth patch

14

near the elbow where you rest it upon the desk?'

'Well, but China?'

'The fish that you have tattooed immediately above your right wrist could only have been done in China. I have made a small study of tattoo marks and have even contributed to the literature of the subject. That trick of staining the fishes' scales a delicate pink is quite peculiar to China. When, in addition, I see a Chinese coin hanging from your watchchain, the matter becomes even more simple.'

Mr. Jabez Wilson laughed heavily. 'Well, I never!' said he. 'I thought at first that you had done something clever, but I see that there was nothing in it, after all.'[1]

Handout

_____

ELEMENTARY, MY DEAR WATSON

QUESTIONS:

1. What is this person's physical appearance?

2. What is this person wearing?

3. What approximate age is this person?

4. What might this person's occupation be? Why?

5. To what economic bracket does this person appear to belong? Why?

6. What kind of personality [pleasant, impatient, sad] does this person appear to have? Why?

7. What other information can you add about this person [place of residence, family status, hobbies, personal habits]?

RULES:

1. You are not to bother your subject in any way.

2. You are to remain completely inconspicuous.

_____

1. Excerpted from *The Complete Sherlock Holmes* by Sir Arthur Conan Doyle. Reprinted by permission of John Lawton Squire and Sheldon Reynolds.

3. You must observe your subject for at least 20 minutes. If a chosen subject cannot be watched for the full 20 minutes, you must choose a new subject.

4. You may follow your subject, if it is convenient for you to do so, as long as you remain inconspicuous and cause no disturbance of any kind.

5. You may listen to any conversations the subject has and engage him or her in casual conversation as long as you can do so pleasantly and without revealing your purpose.

ACTIVITY

Read the description of Holmes' observations to the class.

Then tell the students they are to try their hand at the same thing by going to a busy public place [department store, supermarket, public library, fast food place, waiting room at a hospital, welfare office, or other government agency]. There they are to inconspicuously examine the people and choose one who looks interesting. They are to observe that person for at least 20 minutes and try to answer the questions listed on the handout sheet.

Review both the questions and the rules on the handout sheet with the class.

Tell the students that after they have answered the questions they are to organize their observations under one coherent theme and to write an essay about the person. They can do this in either of two ways:

1. Develop and support a personal point of view about the subject. [He looks like a cheerful person because the corners of his mouth and eyes are surrounded by smile lines.]

2. Select and narrate an illuminating incident involving the subject. [Describe the time you saw your young subject picking on several smaller children not in the playground.]

SPECIAL POINTS

This assignment gets students out of the classroom and into their communities in an exciting way. Most students greatly enjoy playing the role

16

of a private detective or spy. Be sure to allow classroom time for students to report on their experiences as many will have amusing and ingenious tales to tell.

Do this assignment only with a class you can trust to obey the rules. If a number of students suddenly pop up in public places, harass the occupants, and then say it is all for so-and-so's writing class, the consequences could be remarkably unpleasant.

We usually give this assignment on a Thursday and make it due the following Monday. On Friday we check up on the class's weekend surveillance plans to make sure the various plans are reasonable and to give a bit of encouragement to any timid souls who may not know how to proceed.

To help the students organize their essays, you may wish to distribute the handout on outlines, page 191.

We tell the students to work singly rather than in pairs or groups because it is much easier for one person to remain inconspicuous.

In some places it is best for a student to linger by an entrance and to pick a newcomer to observe in order to be fairly certain of a 20 minute surveillance time. Most people who enter a large department store, for example, will shop there for at least 20 minutes. If a student starts following someone who is already well inside the store, he may find his subject has almost finished and will leave before the 20 minutes are up.

Although it seems quite obvious, we tell the students to be sure not to take any chances in doing the assignment: no racing across traffic lanes or subway tracks, no wandering down deserted alleys, no wild driving. We feel it necessary to temper enthusiasm with caution, and so far haven't lost a single student to this assignment.

TUG OF WAR

PURPOSE AND DESCRIPTION

A lively classroom exercise demonstrating the power of imagination and controlled recollection. Particularly useful for those students who write very little about a given topic. Students have a real tug of war with an imaginary rope. Then they write an essay describing a physical activity in which they have participated.

LEVEL   Any.

CLASS PERIODS   Part of one.

ADVANCE PREPARATION   None.

ACTIVITY

The object of this exercise is to have a real tug of war with an imaginary rope. The purpose of this exercise is to have each student imagine the rope so powerfully that it will seem real.

The key to success is to impress on each student the need to concentrate as completely as possible on the nonexistent rope. You can facilitate this concentration by telling the students, "See the rope! Feel the rope! Know it is there! Feel how big it is in your hands—how taut it is—how tightly you are pulling it!"

We introduce this exercise by telling the class we are going to have a tug of war and then bringing out the imaginary rope. The better actor you are, the easier it is for your students to grasp the concept and successfully imagine the rope. So begin by imagining the rope yourself. Feel it, lift it, smell it, coil it, be aware of its shape and weight. Concentrate on it, and you will quickly find that the rope will become real for you and for your students.

Now divide the class in half; pass the rope ends to the two teams; and let the students have a tug of war. Constantly exhort them to concentrate on the rope and feel its reality. At the end of the tug of war some students may even say they have rope burns.

After the tug of war, discuss the rope with the class. Those who really concentrated on it will be able to tell you its color, texture, weight, length, and more.

Explain to the students that they have just seen a demonstration of the power of their concentration, imagination, and recollection. These same tools can also be used in their writing to produce vivid descriptions of events, people, and places they have seen. Such an approach will significantly improve the quality of their writing.

For homework, ask each student to write an essay employing these techniques. Have students describe a physical activity in such a way that the reader will experience it almost physically. Students must write about an activity in which they have actually participated in order to use their own "muscle memory" to select accurate and vivid sensory detail. Descriptions of the location may be included if they enhance the description of the physical activity. Some sample topics: a ten-mile hike in the desert, dancing in a Charleston marathon, pitching with the bases loaded, skiing on a sub-zero day, competing in the 100 yard dash.

SPECIAL POINTS

Do this exercise only if you yourself can see the rope. Only if it works for you will it work for your students.

If you wish to use a second demonstration of the power of concentration and imagination, try this exercise called Jump Rope. Ask for two volunteers. Bring out an imaginary rope once again. This time tell the two students that they are each to take an end and become "turners" of a jump rope. Ask the two students to feel the weight of the rope, and then to turn it in unison, each student's arm making the same size circle, each student's arm in the same place at the same time in the circle as his partner's arm. Ask them to feel the rope slap the ground as it comes around. Their bodies should begin to move with the rhythm of the rope. If the turners are concentrating on the rope and on each other's movements the rope should be almost tangible. At this point ask the class if they can "see" the rope. If they can, ask for a volunteer to jump in and skip rope. Again the jumper must concentrate on the turners' movements and rhythm. If all three students concentrate, the class should be able to tell if the jumper is skipping the rope or if he is missing. Other students may want to skip rope. You can have two students jumping at one time, moving in and out of the rope. Be sure to call a "miss" if a jumper loses the rhythm of the turners and jumps when the imaginary rope is not hitting the ground. Be sure to ask other students to turn or to jump. Even if students do not participate actively in the exercise, they will be able to "see" the rope and the effects that such concentration and imagination can produce.[1]

---

1. This exercise, like the related exercise "Concentration," was derived from *Improvisation for the Theater* by Viola Spolin (Evanston, Illinois: Northwestern University Press, 1963).

CHILDHOOD PHOTOS

PURPOSE AND DESCRIPTION

To help students see how feelings and judgments shape descriptions. Students write about themselves and each other based on early childhood photos.

LEVEL   Any.

CLASS PERIODS   Two.

ADVANCE PREPARATION

Ask each student to bring to class an early childhood photo of himself in which he is at least three years old. If a student has only fairly recent photographs of himself, ask him to bring in the one which shows him at the earliest age. The photo each student brings of himself may include other people. Stress that the photo should *not* be an invaluable family heirloom. Begin this exercise only when every student has a photo.

ACTIVITY   Day One

Ask each student to write his name lightly on the back of the photograph. Collect all the photos and pass them out randomly so that no student has his own. Allow at least 30 minutes for students to describe in writing what they see in the photographs you have given them. They may use any number of approaches [objective description, narration, or interpretation of feelings and relationships based on what they see in the photos]. Whatever approach they choose, they need to pay attention to facial expressions, body positions, hair styles, clothing, any objects included, and the setting. They should also consider whether the photograph is formally arranged, casually arranged, or candid. At the end of the 30 minutes collect the photographs and the descriptions. Return the photos to their owners but keep the written descriptions and bring these to the next day's class.

As homework, ask the students to write about their own photographs by paying close attention to physical detail, and also by drawing from their memory of their lives at the time the photograph was taken. Explain that in this part of the assignment they must again describe what they see, but this time their descriptions should be based on recollection as well as observation. They may want to give themselves more than 30 minutes for this homework part of the exercise. Ask them to bring their photographs and descriptions back for the next day's class.

Day Two

Return to each author, uncorrected, the description he wrote the previous day of someone else's photograph. Have students share both assignments in class. One way to do this is to have the students read in pairs, so that one student reads his description of someone else's photograph, and then the subject of that photograph reads his description of his own picture. In this way, two descriptions of the same photo will be read, one after the other, and the students will be able to compare the similarities and differences in what the two writers saw and interpreted. If students will handle the pictures carefully, you might want to pass around each photograph before both descriptions of it are read. If you have access to an opaque projector, use it to show everyone the photo while the two descriptions are being read.

The first description from each pair will be based solely on observation while the second one will include direct memory as well. Often, students writing about another's picture will pick out details the owner of the picture never observed. One student might describe himself in a photograph as "suffering through another one of those grey, dismal family picnics." Another student, looking at that same photograph, might point out the heavy shadows on the smiling faces, an indication that the picnic was a happy occasion held on a bright sunny day. Speculate with the class as to why these discrepancies in descriptions occur.

Ask the students to compare the tones of each pair of descriptions. Do the two writers have widely differing attitudes toward their shared subject matter? Often the subjective writer's tone will be easier to identify than the objective writer's tone. In each description have students look for key words which communicate the writer's feelings or judgments about his observations. ["A twisted *ugly* tricycle lies *abandoned* in the dirt."] Help the class see how feelings and judgments combined with observations lead the students to make interpretations about the photos and about themselves. Point out that full, interesting description requires this kind of interpretation.

SPECIAL POINTS

This exercise also provides a dramatic example of what can happen in the transition between first person and third person point of view. It illuminates the difference between outside observation and personal involvement.

CHARACTERS

PURPOSE AND DESCRIPTION

A basic preparatory exercise to introduce beginning classes to description. An exercise in noticing details and understanding their implications. Students role-play characters and discuss together how the characterizations were achieved.

LEVEL   Beginning (especially for younger students).

CLASS PERIODS   One.

ADVANCE PREPARATION   None.

ACTIVITY

Tell the students that they are going to participate in a demonstration showing how small details are the elements which make up our understanding of people and places. We pick up verbal, visual, tactile, and auditory clues which we then assemble to form an idea about something or someone.

Look around the room and point out students' various postures and ask what inner feelings they might suggest. Then conduct a brief role-playing scene of the following nature: Ask five student volunteers to sit on five chairs lined up to face the class to represent a bench at a bus stop. Tell them to assume characters of their own choosing. They should try to give the character a name, a profession, an activity from which they have just come, and a place to which they are going. Now ask them to close their eyes and to let their bodies feel the age of the character which they have chosen. Starting with their heads and working toward their feet have them consciously assume the posture and level of energy or tension (or lack thereof) appropriate to this character. Next, have them open their eyes. Then tell them that they are waiting for a bus and that, in the manner of their waiting, they should express their character's age, particular interests, history, and problems. Tell them that they do not know each other, and that for the first minute or so the waiting is to be done without talking. When you feel that these characters have established their identities to the observing class (about 2 minutes), tell them they

24

may speak if they wish, and allow another few minutes for the scene. If a scene develops some dramatic potential, allow it to be acted out fully before you call "curtain." This role playing can then be used as a basis for talking about observing character. Discuss with the class which particular elements [gestures, movements, words] were essential in understanding who each of these five characters was.

SPECIAL POINTS

This exercise is a useful beginning activity in the observation and use of telling detail. Both skills are essential for good descriptive writing. Follow this exercise with "Portrait", page 66, or "A Place in School", page 29.

Classic photographs of people [portraits by Karsh, Cartier-Bresson, Steichen, Avedon] can also be used to develop careful observation. Use an opaque projector to project these photographs onto a screen. As described in *ACTIVITY* above, discuss with the class which details in the portrait are particularly revealing about the person. In the photographs, clothing, location and color also may be indicative of character.

QUICK STUDY

PURPOSE AND DESCRIPTION

To permit students to analyze and improve their powers of observation and retention. Students are shown a variety of objects for a short period of time and are then asked to write a list of as many as they can remember, describing each in as much detail as possible. They are then allowed to examine the objects at their leisure in order to compare them with their written list.

LEVEL   Any.

CLASS PERIODS   One.

ADVANCE PREPARATION

You will need some kind of tray, removable desk drawer, or cardboard box in which to display the objects. (For particularly large classes, see SPECIAL POINTS.) Use an opaque material to cover the box before and after the time during which the class is permitted to view the contents (any kind of covering will do—raincoat, pillow case, newspaper). Put a large number and variety of small objects in the container. In addition to the usual [keys, coins, pencils, rings] try to add a few unusual objects. A dental retainer, old postcard, tiny carving, or obscure piece of electrical or mechanical hardware will provide an interesting contrast. Before the class begins, arrange 10 or so objects in the box and cover it up.

ACTIVITY

Tell the class that you are going to show them some objects in a box for a short period of time. They may not take any notes while they are looking at the objects. When the time is up, they are to write a list of as many as they can remember, describing each in as much detail as possible. After all lists have been completed, show them the box again so they can compare its contents with their written lists.

Have the class look at the box in groups of 10 so that each student has an equal opportunity to view the contents of the box. Permit them to look at the contents for a fixed and short period of time (30 to 60 sec-

26

onds), cover the box, and ask them to prepare their lists. They should attempt to write a detailed description of each object contained in the box. Repeat the exercise several times, using new objects each time. As the students grow more adept, you can increase the number of objects, decrease the observation time, and/or increase the complexity of description required [color, size, function, relationship, degree of wear].

As homework, ask each student to go into a room where he has never been before. He is to spend exactly 2 minutes observing the room without taking any notes. Then he is to leave that room and immediately write as detailed a description of it as he can, using as many sensory details as possible. When he has finished describing it, he should return to the room and assess, in writing, the accuracy of his original description. Tell students to note both the kinds of things they remembered and those they did not [I remembered colors but not smells].

SPECIAL POINTS

If you have a particularly large or unruly class, the same exercise can be done by projecting slides on a screen. An advantage of this approach is that a large number of students will be equally able to see the slides without pushing or standing on chairs. When possible, however, we prefer to use real, three-dimensional objects rather than photographic images.

This exercise provides a useful opportunity to discuss observation in general and observational techniques in particular. After you have repeated the exercise several times, stop the class and ask each student to share his particular observational techniques with his peers. Does he rely on color? Size? Degree of familiarity or unfamiliarity? Does he take a mental photograph? Does he hear his own voice repeating the list of what he has seen? Some students need to do something physical [pace, tap the desk, nod their head] to firmly implant a list in their memory. Students will be particularly interested in the techniques of those who remember the most. Encourage those with weaker powers of recollection to experiment with the techniques used by the more successful ones. Often students will improve dramatically.

You may also wish to ask the class to determine which objects the group as a whole found hardest to remember. Are ordinary thumbtacks or colorful miniature paintings more likely to be recalled?

Plan ahead to make sure you can cope with the mechanical details of this exercise. You will need a surprisingly large number of objects. One good device is to pass the box (covered) around the class and ask each student to add one object of his own. Make sure nothing breakable, live, or temptingly valuable is added. Check the container before showing its contents to the class to make sure each object is adequately exposed.

A good follow-up to this exercise is "The Dispute," page 144.

A PLACE IN SCHOOL

PURPOSE AND DESCRIPTION

An exercise which provides practice in selecting detail for description. Together the students characterize their classroom with descriptive detail. Then, on their own, students take notes at a place on the school campus and write a description of that place.

LEVEL   Beginning.

CLASS PERIODS   One.

ADVANCE PREPARATION   None.

ACTIVITY

To provide some experience in characterizing a place, tell the students to look at the classroom in which you are meeting. Ask a volunteer for a general statement about the room's atmosphere or mood. [This room is colorless. This room helps me think.] If the rest of the class agrees with this general statement, ask the students to supply a list of details about the contents of the room which support the volunteer's characterization and record them on the chalkboard. When this is done, ask the students to supply several descriptive words about each detail. These words should have connotations which strengthen the point of view expressed in the general statement. [If the general statement is that "the room is in poor condition," and one specific detail on the list is "an old chair," the student might supply such words as "shabby," "threadbare," or "dilapidated."]

Repeat this exercise using other general statements from new volunteers.

Now tell students that they are to use their skills in choosing pertinent and vivid detail to write a description of a specific place in school. Discuss some of the possibilities with them [the cafeteria, the locker room, the auditorium, a teacher's classroom which expresses his or her character, a corner of the lawn where a group meets for lunch, a gang's hangout in the parking lot, a hallway at a certain time]. Tell them their papers should have a clear point of view about the character or mood of the place they select. Instruct them to support their point of view by well chosen specifics. No matter how familiar with these places students are, they should return to them to take notes before they write the papers.

SPECIAL POINTS

The fact that the locations described are places experienced by everyone in the class can lead to energetic discussion about differences in points of view. This is because students with differing points of view will have used words with different connotations to describe the same thing. ["The cafeteria is filled with warm, friendly, laughing people." vs. "The cafeteria is crammed with loud, hostile, jostling crowds."] Be sure students have a chance to share these papers with one another.

This exercise is a good preface to the following exercise, "High Tension."

HIGH TENSION

PURPOSE AND DESCRIPTION
An exercise in observation and the selection of detail to set a mood. Students observe people in a place where emotions are close to the surface, take notes on their observations, and then organize their material into a descriptive essay which emphasizes mood and atmosphere.

LEVEL   Any.

CLASS PERIODS   One-quarter plus one to two.

ADVANCE PREPARATION   None.

ACTIVITY   Day One

Take the last 10 to 15 minutes of a class period to give this assignment.

Discuss with your class the idea that close observation is essential to good writing. The gestures, voices, odors, words, clothes, and postures of people, and the colors, noises, shapes, textures, movement, and temperature of a place are the details which paint a vivid picture and give the reader an impression of a person or a place.

Tell the students they are to choose a place outside of the classroom in which emotions are close to the surface [a hospital, a dentist's or doctor's waiting room, an unemployment office, an airport, bus, or train station, the scene of an athletic contest, a principal's office, a classroom before, during, or after an important examination, a traffic court]. Each student should spend at least one hour at his chosen location taking notes on his surroundings. His notes should consist of carefully observed detail of the sort mentioned above. He should try to note the intangible mood of the place as well as the tangible detail. The students are to have a week outside of class time in which to complete this assignment. When their notes are complete, either have the students write the essay described below at home, or in class on Day Two.

Day Two

Hold a workshop in class so that students can organize their notes and begin to write with your help. Ask each student to refer to his notes to

31

determine what general mood or feeling characterizes the place he selected. Then ask each student to write an essay with the central purpose of conveying the general mood or feeling of his chosen place. In organizing the essay, the student should select from his notes those details which will best express that mood or feeling. He should be careful to select descriptive words with connotations that convey the same mood or feeling. If he feels a dentist's waiting room is a frightening place, he might choose such words and phrases as "forbidding," "filled with the acrid smell of nervous perspiration," or "menaced by the high-pitched whine of the distant drill."

Day Three

Have the students share their essays. In the ensuing discussion make sure that the students consider the quality of detail in each paper and how well it supported the paper's central purpose.

SPECIAL POINTS

The optional workshop for Day Two provides an opportunity to guide work in progress. The organization of the kind of notes which this assignment calls for is often a very difficult job for students. It helps if you are there when they are going through the organizing process. To further assist them in organizing their notes, you may wish to distribute the handout on outlines, page 183.

For advanced students you can ask that the mood conveyed by the writer be implicit in the selection and organization of detail and not directly stated to the reader in an introductory thesis paragraph.

When you give this assignment, mention to the students that even though they may not see obvious or dramatic displays of emotion in the place where they observe, this does not mean that "nothing is happening here." Urge them to look for small signs of tension, the various ways people cover anxiety or impatience, the physical clues to deeper feelings. You may want to refer to the many recent studies done on body language.

The observer-spy-detective role has a quality of adventure about it. This kind of active observation sensitizes students to telling detail and heightens their awareness of how to look at something, and what to look for.

Students like to share these essays in class. They are curious about where their classmates went and what they saw.

Useful exercises to precede this one are "A Place in School," page 29; "Portrait," page 66; and, for younger students, "Characters," page 24. "Elementary, My Dear Watson," page 14, can be a good follow-up to this assignment.

THE ORANGE

PURPOSE AND DESCRIPTION

To encourage students to use all five senses in descriptive writing. Students take descriptive notes on an orange: first from a distance, then close up, then after it is cut into a flower configuration, and, finally, after they eat segments of it. Using these notes, they write a description of the orange, making as full use as possible of their five senses.

LEVEL   Beginning and intermediate.

CLASS PERIODS   One to two.

ADVANCE PREPARATION

You will need one orange for every eight students, a sharp knife, and a number of paper towels.

ACTIVITY   Day One

Bring the oranges, knife, and paper towels to class, hidden from the students' view.

Arrange the students in circles of eight. Then follow this sequence for each circle. Place one orange in the middle of the circle of students. Tell the students that they are going to use the object in the center of their circle to practice using their five senses in description. The first sense they will use in describing it will be sight.

Tell the students that each of them sees the object from a slightly different viewpoint, and that each of them is to describe the object from his own viewpoint. Remind them to describe its size, shape, color, texture, and position as accurately and fully as they can. Give the students five minutes for this description.

After five minutes, give the orange to one student in the circle. Tell him he may now add three more senses—touch, smell, and hearing—to his sense of sight in order to perceive and then to describe the object. Give the student up to 30 seconds to hold, smell, tap, and look closely at the orange, and then ask him to pass it to the person on his right so that each student may in turn perceive the orange with these additional

34

senses. As soon as each student passes the orange, he should write down any new descriptive details he has seen, smelled, felt, or heard.

After all the students have described the orange this second time, place the orange on several paper towels on a table, desk, or chair in the circle so that the orange is clearly visible to all the students in the circle. Place the orange so the navel or stem point is straight up. Through this point cut almost through the orange so that it is divided into two equal parts. Be sure to cut through the meat of the orange but not all the way through the skin on the opposite side so that the two halves are still connected by the skin. Then make the same kind of cut at right angles to the first cut so that the orange is now divided in quarters. Cut the orange two more times in the same manner so that it is divided into eight equal slices, all still attached by the skin at the bottom of the orange. Now spread each of the eighths away from the middle so that the orange opens up as a flower would, the slices resembling petals. Place the orange again in the middle of the circle and ask the students to describe what they now see. Tell them to use whichever of their senses seems appropriate to this description. Also tell them they may want to compare and/or contrast the object to other objects in order to describe it fully. Again, give the students five minutes to write these descriptions.

At the end of the third round of description, cut the orange all the way through the last bit of skin that held the eight pieces together and give one section to each student in each circle. Tell the students that they may now apply their five senses to the object in whatever way they choose. Give them five minutes again to write any new descriptive details to which they may now have access concerning the orange.

When the students have completed this fourth phase of description, and you and they have cleaned up any last remnants of the oranges, tell them that they should now have extensive sensory data on the object. For homework ask them to use the data to write a description of the object—making as full use as possible of the notes they took during the classroom exercise. Tell them that they may rearrange their information in any order they wish and that they need not even refer to the class-room exercise but that they must make use of all five senses in their paragraphs. Remind the students that each paragraph needs a topic sentence which states a point of view and which determines what information the rest of the paragraph will include.

Day Two: (optional)

Have students share their descriptions in class. Since they have all based their descriptions on similar sensory data, they may enjoy hearing the very different ways each of them chose to arrange his information. Have the students comment on which senses each writer most effectively used in his description and which details most captured the listener's attention.

Have the students hand in both the notes taken during the classroom exercise and the description written for homework.

SPECIAL POINTS

We do not call the orange by its name to the students during the exercise because we want every descriptive detail to come from them, even its name. If students ask if they may use its name, we say yes and explain that names are often essential elements in description.

Whether or not you decide to have the students share their descriptions in class, be sure to ask them to hand in both the notes taken during the classroom exercise and the descriptions written for homework. We ask for both to see what use the students made of their sensory data.

If some students simply recopy the notes they took in class for their description, ask them to rewrite, focusing each paragraph with a topic sentence and, if possible, drawing from all four parts of their notes for each paragraph.

THE EGG

PURPOSE AND DESCRIPTION:

An exercise to demonstrate how specific sensory detail and a variety of other stylistic devices enrich description. Students watch the teacher fry an egg, write a description of what they observed, read a description from James Joyce, then rewrite their own description.

LEVEL   Advanced.

CLASS PERIODS   Two.

ADVANCE PREPARATION

Bring an egg, a frying pan, a spatula, some butter, and an electric hot plate to class.

Handout

_____

FROM *ULYSSES*, BY JAMES JOYCE

———Scald the teapot.

On the boil sure enough: a plume of steam from the spout. He scalded and rinsed out the teapot and put in four full spoons of tea, tilting the kettle then to let water flow in. Having set it to draw, he took off the kettle and crushed the pan flat on the live coals and watched the lump of butter slide and melt. While he unwrapped the kidney the cat mewed hungrily against him. Give her too much meat she won't mouse. Say they won't eat pork. Kosher. Here. He let the blood-smeared paper fall to her and dropped the kidney amid the sizzling butter sauce. Pepper. He sprinkled it through his fingers, ringwise, from the chipped eggcup. . . . (He then goes upstairs and brings breakfast tea to his wife.)

. . . .

———There's a smell of burn, she said. Did you leave anything on the fire?

———The kidney! he cried suddenly.

37

He fitted the book roughly into his inner pocket and, stubbing his toes against the broken commode, hurried out towards the smell, stepping hastily down the stairs with a flurried stork's legs. Pungent smoke shot in an angry jet from the side of the pan. By prodding a prong of the fork under the kidney he detached it and turned it turtle on its back. Only a little burned. He tossed it off the pan on to a plate and let the scanty brown gravy trickle over it.

Cup of tea now. He sat down, cut and buttered a slice of the loaf. He shore away the burnt flesh and flung it to the cat. Then he put a forkful into his mouth, chewing with discernment the toothsome pliant meat. Done to a turn. A mouthful of tea. Then he cut away dies of bread, sopped one in the gravy and put it in his mouth.[1]

ACTIVITY   Day One:

Tell the class that they are to watch all that you do very carefully, paying special attention to as many details as possible, and that they are then to write a description of what they have seen. Next, without comment, fry the egg. Students who don't complete their descriptive paragraphs may finish them at home.

Day Two:

Begin class the following day by distributing the Joyce handout. Tell the students to read the passage once, and to ask for definitions of any words they do not know.

Then ask them to read the passage a second time, noting in the margin the senses Joyce played upon in his description and underlining the places where the description seems particularly vivid. Tell them that vivid description is created not only by the use of sensory detail, but also by a variety of stylistic devices which will become clear as the passage is discussed in class.

Now, in class discussion have the students point out the places where the description was especially vivid. List on the board the names for the stylistic devices these places exemplify. Besides sensory detail, your list might include point of view, emphasis, shortened sentence pattern, quality of the verbs and adverbs, metaphor, repetition, and onomatopoeia.

During this discussion, also point out that Joyce's combination of narration with description allows him to comprehend all the activity of the episode—what the character thinks, what he does, and what he feels. Suggest that your students, in order to expand their points of view, might want to incorporate this combination in their own writing.

For homework, have each student select two devices, other than sensory detail, from those listed on the board. Have students note those devices, along with the words *sensory detail*, in the margin of their descriptions of the class egg-frying episode. Now tell them to concentrate on the use of the three devices written in the margin and to revise their paragraphs. Have them hand in both the first draft and the revision on the following day.

SPECIAL POINTS

This assignment is only for those writers sophisticated enough to understand Joyce's use of sentence fragments and stream of consciousness. Because many of our students have too eagerly plunged into a style of cryptic fragments, we are careful to explain the fragment's limited effectiveness.

Often students will concentrate on describing the egg or on relating the entire egg-frying incident without seeing the possibility of combining detailed description with a narrative of the whole event. So we have to remind them of the benefit derived from combining narrative and descriptive techniques.

We emphasize to our students that we do not offer the Joyce passage as a model against which they must compare their own efforts. Rather, we want them to use this passage as a source of stylistic devices from which they may enrich their own store of writing techniques.

This exercise also demonstrates the benefits of rereading and rewriting.

We have found these two follow-up assignments especially successful:

1. Have students write a description of an entire meal—using sensory detail to produce an experience for the reader close to each student's own experience of the meal. Ask students to pay particular attention to color, smell, texture, and shape. Tell them to describe not only the food, but also its setting as a part of the experience—the room, the table, the noise in the room, the atmosphere in general, and the people.

You may want to assign this essay near a holiday such as Thanksgiving or Easter. However, an ordinary breakfast, a fast food lunch, or a TV dinner can also be an effective subject for this essay.

2. Tell students that they are to eat something they have never eaten before and to describe the food and the experience of eating it in an essay. Tell them that they must pay careful attention to sensory detail in the essay—recreating the experience for the reader through use of this detail. Suggest that students eat the new food slowly, giving themselves time to absorb each aspect of the new experience before writing their description.

THE PENNY

PURPOSE AND DESCRIPTION

A group activity done in class to demonstrate subtle distinctions among words. The teacher draws a penny on the chalkboard following instructions from the class. The challenge to the students is to make the instructions so specific that the teacher draws precisely what they want.

LEVEL Beginning.

CLASS PERIODS   One.

ADVANCE PREPARATION

Have each student bring a penny to class. Bring a few extra pennies yourself because one or two students are sure to forget.

ACTIVITY

Tell the students that you are going to draw a penny on the board according to their instructions. Explain that you are a robot and will follow their instructions *exactly*. Say that your programming has only just begun, and at this point you know only the parts of your body, the board, and the chalk. They will have to teach you all the other things you will need to know in order to draw a penny properly. Once you have been "taught" a concept—such as *up*, or the letter T—you will remember it.

Tell the students to decide among themselves which side of the penny they want you to draw. Let them determine their own organization and method of attack.

Follow their instructions exactly. Try to draw something other than what they wish you to draw if it is at all possible to so misinterpret their instructions. They should catch on quickly and will have great fun working out extremely precise commands.

SPECIAL POINTS

This exercise demonstrates the superiority of precise language to vague language. It serves as a useful reference point in later classes or conferences when you discuss the need for precision.

41

Because successful completion of the exercise requires group cooperation, this exercise can be used to unify students in a class. It is also a good exercise to try when a class feels stale and needs a change.

We have the teacher pretend such extreme ignorance because the process of describing fundamental concepts—such as a circle—is particularly challenging. In fact, the definition and construction of a large circle can take a class 15 minutes or more.

A COMMON OBJECT

PURPOSE AND DESCRIPTION

A class or small group activity which offers practice in moving from the general to the particular in description, in subordinating ideas, and in presenting ideas in order of importance. A student describes an ordinary object and the class draws it. The resulting drawings are used to evaluate the accuracy of the description.

LEVEL   Beginning and intermediate.

CLASS PERIODS   One.

ADVANCE PREPARATION

Bring, in a paper bag, as many small, simply designed, and familiar objects as there are students in the class [a paper clip, a safety pin, a jack from a game of jacks, a softball, a nail file, a comb].

ACTIVITY

Ask the students to have scratch paper in front of them. Give an object from the bag to a volunteer, and ask him to hide the object from the view of the other students. Without showing his object, have the volunteer describe it in detail so that the class can draw it using his description. He is not allowed to tell what object he is describing. He may use measurement and metaphor to describe the object. The students are to draw *exactly* what they hear in the order in which they hear it. After the description, have the sketchers hold their drawings up for the class and the describing student to analyze.

If the description is precise, the drawing on each student's paper should reproduce the object accurately and to life size. If the describing student starts with an unimportant detail and moves from the particular to the general, he will find that the sketches are inaccurate and disproportionate. If he neglects size or overall shape before he moves to small detail, the sketches will be all sizes. Based on the variations in the drawings, discuss as a group where the description was inaccurate.

Repeat this exercise several times, each time letting a different student describe a different object. Then divide the students into smaller groups of four or five to repeat the procedure. In this way, each student will have a chance to describe an object and to have his description evaluated by other students.

SPECIAL POINTS

Follow-up discussion helps the student who has just described his object understand the inaccuracies in his description. It also helps him to reorganize his information. For instance, he may realize that if he had begun: "This is a six-sided figure 2 inches in diameter . . .," rather than: "Draw a diagonal line ¼–inch long . . .," he could have avoided many of the errors in the drawings.

We give each of the students an object, rather than have them fish in the bag. In that way, we conceal the identity of the objects not yet described.

This is a particularly good exercise for visually oriented students. It helps them perceive the gap between visual perception and the verbal description of that perception, and emphasizes the need to close that gap through a careful, accurate choice of words.

The preceding exercise, "The Penny," is closely related to this one. In "The Penny" the class works as a group to describe an object so that the teacher, following the students' directions, will draw the object accurately. In "A Common Object" each student makes a drawing based on the description of one student. Each individual describes once and draws several times. The experience of trying to draw from descriptions which are incomplete and confusing makes students more careful when they choose descriptive detail in future essays.

It is a good idea to use "The Penny" first if you choose to use both of these exercises. When students see, in "The Penny," how careless description can produce confusion, they will be more careful when they present their descriptions for "A Common Object."

44

HOW TO

PURPOSE AND DESCRIPTION

To exercise students' powers of description by practicing economy of language and sequential accumulation of detail. Students are asked to write careful and accurate instructions which will teach someone how to do something for the first time. Then students actually follow the instructions.

LEVEL   Beginning and intermediate.

CLASS PERIODS   One-quarter plus one.

ADVANCE PREPARATION   None.

ACTIVITY   Day One

Provide 10 minutes at the *end* of a class period to give this assignment.

For homework ask students to think of a task which is useful, which they sincerely enjoy doing, and which not everyone knows how to do [baiting a hook, cutting hair, arranging flowers]. Then ask them to instruct, in writing, a novice in the art of whatever task they have chosen to describe. Remind them that they must be clear, logical, and include all the necessary information and detail a novice would need. Tell them that tomorrow someone in the class will have to depend on their written instructions alone to perform, for the first time, whatever task they have described. Also ask them to bring in, if necessary, any special materials required to engage in the activity. Flower arranging, for instance, would require a vase and some flowers. Obviously students should not choose to give instructions for something which would be impossible to do in the classroom. Skydiving instructions, for example, would be inappropriate.

Day Two

At the beginning of class have each student name the task he has described in writing. Then ask a student to volunteer to follow someone else's instructions in front of the class. Be sure that the volunteer is really

45

a novice and has not had any experience with the task he has volunteered to complete.

Ask a second student to read the instructions to the volunteer as he performs his task so that the volunteer will not be slowed down by having to read them repeatedly to himself. Do not allow the writer of the instructions to read them to the volunteer because he might be tempted to add something verbally which he did not include in the original text. Stress that the writer of the instructions must be mute while the volunteer is performing, but that during this time he should write down any bits of information he realizes he has left out.

The volunteer may at no time ask the writer of the instructions or anyone else to clarify or explain them. If the volunteer is confused, urge him to do his best and to do what he *thinks* the instructions mean. Only if he finds the instructions completely incomprehensible may he stop before completing the task. In that case, another volunteer may assist the student who is not able to follow the instructions. Be sure a class discussion follows each completed task and includes speculations and observations concerning any misinterpretations the volunteer made in the process of following the instructions, as well as any information the writer of the instructions realizes he left out.

After the class has witnessed at least one volunteer complete a set of instructions and has followed that performance with a discussion, you may want to break the activity into smaller groupings so that as many sets of instructions as possible can be performed and evaluated. In that case, match up a number of volunteers with instructions and appropriate materials. Then divide the class into smaller sections, each section grouped around a volunteer novice working on a task.

After a number of students have followed one another's instructions, in a class discussion compare the various approaches writers took to describe their tasks. Did any general trends emerge? How did the descriptions differ? Were any details extraneous? Was the order of details logical? Sequential?

If you intend to collect these papers, at the end of the class ask each student whose instructions were performed to include, at the bottom of his paper, those points or details which he realized he omitted in the original text. During the class activity, students whose instructions were not performed may also realize certain omissions they made and may also wish to add points or details to their papers at this time.

SPECIAL POINTS

This assignment requires that students cooperate with and reach out to one another. Since students serve as both writers and followers of instructions, they are able to experience both sides of the process. They learn how to write clear precise instructions, and they also learn to do something they have never done before. Through this exercise we have seen students learn how to make a salad, string a bow, do a pirouette, give a haircut, tool leather, and carve a chicken.

A valuable extension of this exercise is to have the students rewrite their descriptions, this time taking a clear point of view about the process. Each should begin his paper with a thesis statement expressing his point of view. [A spontaneous salad is the height of the saladmaker's art. I get nervous cutting people's hair. Tooling leather is a socially acceptable way to make a mess.] Then, by reworking each piece of information from his original description, he should develop his thesis statement into an essay supporting his thesis. (This is a variation on a suggested essay topic in Sheridan Baker's *The Practical Stylist*. New York: Thomas Y. Crowell Company, 1973.)

2 TECHNIQUES OF ORGANIZATION

This section begins with an exercise demonstrating the functions of the introduction and the conclusion in an essay. Then there are three exercises which give students practice in developing topic sentences, and an exercise demonstrating the connections between topic sentences and the paragraphs which follow. There are also two exercises on developing and supporting a thesis and two exercises to help students gather material for and organize essays of comparison and contrast. We end this section with an exercise which asks students to use three methods (description, narration, and exposition) to develop the same thesis.

INTRODUCTIONS AND CONCLUSIONS

PURPOSE AND DESCRIPTION

A three-day exercise to develop skills of writing introductions and conclusions. Students first examine a short biographical essay. Then, based on an analysis of that essay's structure, they write an introduction; three substantive paragraphs; and, finally, a conclusion to an autobiographical sketch illustrated by a childhood memory.

LEVEL   Any.

CLASS PERIODS   Three.

ADVANCE PREPARATION

1. Bring to class an overhead projector and a copy of the following essay by Charles Schulz, "Snoopy: The Authorized Biography of a Great American."[1] (For advanced students, see SPECIAL POINTS.)

SNOOPY: THE AUTHORIZED BIOGRAPHY
OF A GREAT AMERICAN

It is difficult to write an accurate biography of Snoopy because many of his recollections seem to be marred by fanciful dreams. We are led to believe that he was very active in W.W.I and that he was actually the victim of the accurate gunfire of Baron Von Richtofen on several dramatic occasions. Military records are vague about these encounters.

One thing is sure, however. He was born at the Daisy Hill Puppy Farm. His father's occupation was probably much like that of other beagles. He chased his quota of rabbits and retired early. We know little about his mother, although at one time we almost discovered her whereabouts when Snoopy set off to find her. The high point of that journey was the supposed sighting of his mother and his rushing across a

---

1. *The People's Almanac* by David Wallechinsky and Irving Wallace (Doubleday & Company, Inc., Garden City, New York, 1975, pp 31-32).

field toward a farmyard shouting, "Mom! Mom! Mom!" only to be brought up short when he discovered that it wasn't his mom. He had been deceived by the fact, on his own admission, that to him all beagles look alike.

We are not sure how many brothers and sisters Snoopy has, but we do know that one brother lives in Washington and the other in Texas. One sister lives in St. Louis, one in Hollywood, and one in Kansas. A family reunion was arranged at one time, but it turned out to be rather a letdown. To quote Snoopy, "The anticipation far exceeded the actual event." When he was asked to describe what went on at the reunion, he said that none of them spoke the same language. The years had turned them into strangers. His advice from Lucy, when he felt guilty about being disappointed in the reunion, was simply not to feel guilty about it. "Just because you are related to people," she said, "doesn't mean you have to like them."

Snoopy's memories of the Daisy Hill Puppy Farm seem to be mostly good ones. We are told that he used, especially, to enjoy the beautiful summer evenings. One thing he described was how they sat around and sang, while someone strummed a banjo, although, upon being pressed for details, he admitted that perhaps no one actually played the banjo, and they didn't really sing, but what happened was they merely howled a lot. Snoopy has revisited his birthplace several times, but on his last trip, he was horrified to discover that the Daisy Hill Puppy Farm no longer exists. It has been replaced by a multistoried parking lot. Upon seeing this monstrosity, he cried out, "You stupid people, you're parking on my memories."

His career as a W.W.I flying ace has been replaced with that of a barnstormer. He is also well into a career as a novelist and has had a fair amount of success with the publication of a stirring drama called *It Was a Dark and Stormy Night*. He almost gained immortality as a baseball player when he had the opportunity to become the 1st player to tie Babe Ruth's home-run record of 714 home runs. Unfortunately, in his last time to bat, in the last game of the season,

Charlie Brown got picked off 2nd, thus ending the game, and Snoopy was beaten out by Hank Aaron.

There are many dreams left, and dreams of the future are just as good as dreams of the past. Lying on top of a doghouse enables one, also, to look upward. This is the advantage he has over the rest of us.

The Author: Charles M. Schulz, creator of the memorable comic strip *Peanuts*, has fathered Charlie Brown, Lucy, Linus, and Snoopy.

Handout

HOMEWORK: INTRODUCTIONS

Write a short personal essay. Begin by making a list of ten of your most significant personality traits [giggly, enjoy dancing, eat when nervous]. This list is private, for your use only. After your list is complete, select one trait and write a thesis sentence about it which you will be able to develop through anecdote. For instance: I giggle at the most inappropriate moments.

Next, find an incident or memory from your childhood to illustrate the particular trait you have chosen. Now you know your thesis (the statement about the trait you have selected) and the material you will use to shape your essay (the childhood memory). Using what you have learned about introductions, write an introductory paragraph and list the three main points you will use in the three paragraph body of your essay.

ACTIVITY   Day One

Display the Schulz essay on the overhead projector and have your students read it at least twice, paying special attention to the introductory paragraph. Now discuss how introductions predict, shape, and capsulize a complete essay, and how the topic sentence of an introductory paragraph is the thesis sentence for the entire essay. (See SPECIAL POINTS for a discussion of explicit versus implicit thesis statements.)

Help your students to understand how the whole form and tone of this essay is set in the introductory paragraph—how Schulz establishes the ambiguity and poignancy of Snoopy's life in the first generalization and then through the accompanying facts. Show your students how Schulz guides the reader through the essay by having each paragraph illustrate the theme of the dream-wish in the thesis statement: "It is difficult to write an accurate biography of Snoopy because many of his recollections seem to be marred by fanciful dreams." Point out, too, that Schulz' tone, both compassionate yet incredulous, is clear in the introduction and determines how the reader is to understand and evaluate Snoopy's life.

After the discussion, distribute the homework assignment. Remind students that the introductions to their own essays should try to predict, shape, and capsulize, just as Schulz did in "Snoopy."

Day Two

Ask several students to share with the class their introductions and the main points that will make up their essays. Ask the listeners to evaluate how well the elements of the introduction [thesis statement, point of view, word choice, organization] are related to the list of anecdotes for the main paragraphs. Was there a clear, explicit thesis statement in each introductory paragraph? Where did the thesis statement occur? At the beginning or end of the paragraph? Did an introduction first tantalize the reader with a bit of exciting detail or did it (as in "Snoopy") explain its central idea first and then provide detail to support that idea? Point out that the placement of the thesis depends on the purpose of the essay [personal reminiscence often uses immediate detail to capture a reader's interest, whereas a business report usually begins with clear general statements].

After the discussion, have students begin work in class on the three-paragraph body of the essays which they will finish at home.

Day 3

Begin by having the class look again at the Schulz essay, this time concentrating on the concluding paragraph. Point out that conclusions should expand and enlarge the reader's perspective of the thesis. This can be done in a number of ways. The writer may use one concrete detail to stand for and emphasize a larger abstraction. The writer may move to that larger abstraction through a new general statement, or he may summarize and recapitulate all that has gone before. He may ask a further question or provide an answer. Schulz moves back to his thesis on Snoopy's "fanciful dreams"; then he moves forward a new conclusion—suggesting that dreaming carries Snoopy "upward" and that "this is the advantage that he has over the rest of us."

After this discussion, have each student write a conclusion to his personal reminiscence.

SPECIAL POINTS

We use a very short essay as our model so that we can show the interrelationships between the introduction and the body of the essay again and again. Another important point which a beginning class needs to learn and an advanced class needs to examine in depth is the difference between an explicit and implicit thesis. In his first sentence, Schulz *explicitly* states the thesis that his main paragraphs will *implicitly* illustrate.

With advanced classes you can do this same exercise, but substitute the following excerpt from Alfred Kazin's "The Block and Beyond." (Paragraphs are numbered to facilitate discussion.)

1. The block: *my* block. It was on the Chester Street side of our house, between the grocery and the back wall of the old drugstore, that I was hammered into the shape of the streets. Everything beginning at Blake Avenue would always wear for me some delightful strangeness and mildness, simply because it was not of my block, *the* block, where the clang of your head sounded against the pavement when you fell in a fist fight, and the rows of storelights on each side were pitiless, watching you. Anything away from the block was good: even a school you never went to, two blocks away: there were vegetable gardens in the park across the street. Returning from "New York," I would take the longest routes home from the subway, get off a station ahead of our own, only for the unexpectedness of walking through Betsy Head Park and hearing the gravel crunch under my feet as I went beyond the vegetable gardens, smelling the sweaty sweet dampness from the pool in summer and the dust on the leaves as I passed

under the ailanthus trees. On the block itself everything rose up only to test me.

2. We worked every inch of it, from the cellars and the backyards to the sickening space between the roofs. Any wall, any stoop, any curving metal edge on a billboard sign made a place against which to knock a ball; any bottom rung of a fire escape ladder a goal in basketball; any sewer cover a base; any crack in the pavement a "net" for the tense sharp tennis that we played by beating a soft ball back and forth with our hands between the squares. Betsy Head Park two blocks away would always feel slightly foreign, for it belonged to the Amboys and the Bristols and the Hopkinsons as much as it did to us. *Our* life every day was fought out on the pavement and in the gutter, up against the walls of the houses and the glass fronts of the drugstore and the grocery, in and out of the fresh steaming piles of horse manure, the wheels of passing carts and automobiles, along the iron spikes of the stairway to the cellar, the jagged edge of the open garbage cans, the crumbly steps of the old farmhouses still left on one side of the street.

3. As I go back to the block now, and for a moment fold my body up again in its narrow arena—there, just there, between the black of the asphalt and the old women in their kerchiefs and flowered housedresses sitting on the tawny kitchen chairs—the back wall of the drugstore still rises up to test me. Every day we smashed a small black viciously hard regulation handball against it with fanatical cuts and drives and slams, beating and slashing at it almost in hatred for the blind strength of the wall itself. I was never good enough at handball, was always practicing some trick shot that might earn me esteem, and when I was weary of trying, would often bat a ball down Chester Street just to get myself to Blake Avenue. I have this memory of playing one-o'-cat by myself in the sleepy twilight, at a moment when everyone else had left the block. The sparrows floated down from the telephone wires to peck at every fresh pile of horse manure, and there was a smell of brine from the delicatessen store, of egg crates and of the milk scum left in the great metal cans outside the

grocery, of the thick white paste oozing out from behind the fresh Hecker's Flour ad on the metal signboard. I would throw the ball in the air, hit it with my bat, then with perfect satisfaction drop the bat to the ground and run to the next sewer cover. Over and over I did this, from sewer cover to sewer cover, until I had worked my way to Blake Avenue and could see the park.

4. With each clean triumphant ring of my bat against the gutter leading me on, I did the whole length of our block up and down, and never knew how happy I was just watching the asphalt rise and fall, the curve of the steps up to an old farmhouse. The farmhouses themselves were streaked red on one side, brown on the other, but the steps themselves were always gray. There was a tremor of pleasure at one place; I held my breath in nausea at another. As I ran after my ball with the bat heavy in my hand, the odd successiveness of things in myself almost choked me, the world was so full as I ran—past the cobblestoned yards into the old farmhouses, where stray chickens still waddled along the stones; past the little candy store where we went only if the big one on our side of the block was out of Eskimo pies; past the three neighboring tenements where the last of the old women sat on their kitchen chairs yawning before they went up to make supper. Then came Mrs. Rosenwasser's house, the place on the block I first identified with what was farthest from home, and strangest, because it was a "private" house; then the fences around the monument works, where black cranes rose up above the yard and you could see the smooth gray slabs that would be cut and carved into tombstones, some of them already engraved with the names and dates and family virtues of the dead.

5. Beyond Blake Avenue was the pool parlor outside which we waited all through the tense September afternoons of the World's Series to hear the latest scores called off the ticker tape—and where as we waited, banging a ball against the bottom of the wall and drinking water out of empty coke bottles, I breathed the chalk off the cues and listened to the clocks ringing in the fire station across the street. There was

an old warehouse next to the pool parlor; the oil on the barrels and the iron staves had the same rusty smell. A block away was the park, thick with the dusty gravel I liked to hear my shoes crunch in as I ran round and round the track; then a great open pavilion, the inside mysteriously dark, chill even in summer; there I would wait in the sweaty coolness before pushing on to the wading ring where they put up a shower on the hottest days.

6. Beyond the park the "fields" began, all those still unused lots where we could still play hard ball in perfect peace—first shooing away the goats and then tearing up goldenrod before laying our bases. The smell and touch of those "fields," with their wild compost under the billboards of weeds, goldenrod, bricks, goat droppings, rusty cans, empty beer bottles, fresh new lumber, and damp cement, live in my mind as Brownsville's great open door, the wastes that took us through to the west. I used to go round them in summer with my cousins selling near-beer to the carpenters, but always in a daze, would stare so long at the fibrous stalks of the goldenrod as I felt their harshness in my hand that I would forget to make a sale, and usually go off sick on the beer I drank up myself. Beyond! Beyond! Only to see something new, to get away from each day's narrow battleground between the grocery and the back wall of the drugstore! Even the other end of our block, when you got to Mrs. Rosenwasser's house and the monument works, was dear to me for the contrast. On summer nights, when we played Indian trail, running away from each other on prearranged signals, the greatest moment came when I could plunge into the darkness down the block for myself and hide behind the slabs in the monument works. I remember the air whistling around me as I ran, the panicky thud of my bones in my sneakers, and then the slabs rising in the light from the street lamps as I sped past the little candy store and crept under the fence.

7. In the darkness you could never see where the crane began. We liked to trap the enemy between the slabs and sometimes jumped them from great mounds of rock just in from the quarry. A boy once fell to his death that way, and

they put a watchman there to keep us out. This made the slabs all the more impressive to me, and I always aimed first for that yard whenever we played follow-the-leader. Day after day the monument works became oppressively more mysterious and remote, though it was only just down the block; I stood in front of it every afternoon on my way back from school, filling it with my fears. It was not death I felt there—the slabs were usually faceless. It was the darkness itself, and the wind howling around me whenever I stood poised on the edge of a high slab waiting to jump. Then I would take in, along with the fear, some amazement of joy that I had found my way out that far.[2]

Point out how the thesis statement *explicitly* states "On the block itself everything rose up only to test me." It *implicitly* suggests that "beyond" the block life was more welcoming and less of a battle. The whole essay is built around the comparison and contrast implied in this thesis. And so the structure of the introduction, its word choice and the quality of its detail shape that comparison and contrast. In this essay even the syntax and punctuation ["The block: my block"] develop the cramped feeling Kazin wishes the reader to experience. Show how the body of the essay, like the introductory paragraph, moves from detail inside the block to points further and further away. Then show how in the conclusion Kazin moves further away than he has ever been before, not off the block, but into the "joy" and "fear" of his own imagination.

---

2. From *A Walker in the City*. Copyright, 1951, by Alfred Kazin, Reprinted by permission of Harcourt, Brace Jovanovich, Inc.

COLLECTIVE QUESTIONING

PURPOSE AND DESCRIPTION

To practice formulating generalizations based on specific information and to heighten listening and interpretive skills. A student becomes a character from a recently read book or short story and is interviewed by other members of the class. The rest of the students then make generalizations about the character based on the information they receive in response to their questions. Students must have done independent reading to participate in this exercise. (This is a good introduction to the next exercise, "Self-Portrait," page 63.)

LEVEL   Beginning.

CLASS PERIODS   One.

ADVANCE PREPARATION   None.

ACTIVITY

If possible, arrange the class in a circle. Choose a student who has recently read a novel or short story independent of any required curriculum reading. Tell the student to become a character from that novel or short story. Tell him to sit in his chair as that character would or, if necessary, to choose another position entirely, standing or sitting on the floor perhaps. Suggest that he take on any gestures or expressions of that character which seem appropriate. After the student has had enough time to get into his role, ask him to introduce himself to the group by giving a few basic facts about his character. ["My name is Tom Sawyer. I live in Missouri. I am twelve years old."]

Now it is the other students' responsibility to find out as much as they can about this character, but they may ask only one question each. Remind students to listen carefully to every question before their turn comes so they do not elicit information already given. Also point out that they should use previous questions as springboards for new questions. Remind the interviewee to stay in character at all times.

When each student has asked one question, instruct everyone to write, in one sentence only, the most meaningful generalization he can make about the character interviewed. Tell the students that, to be meaningful, the generalizations must have a point of view and must be broad enough to cover as many details as the interview revealed, yet specific enough to be interesting and to distinguish this character from any other character. ["Tom Sawyer wasn't much of a student, but he managed to get himself in and out of so many dramatic situations that he learned more as a boy than many people learn in their entire lives."] By limiting the generalization to one sentence, you require the students to immediately get to the main point of their observations and interpretations, and to condense them. Remind the students that the behavior of the character during the interview is information as well. Also ask the student who was interviewed to write a one sentence description of the character he played.

Finally, have students read their sentences to the class. Did students receive similar impressions of the character? How did they differ? Why? Did the generalizations emphasize different qualities of the character? Were the generalizations interesting enough to make listeners want to hear more about the character described?

SPECIAL POINTS

Collective questioning becomes more effective if each student pays attention to what has gone before. Usually questions begin quite generally and move toward specific detail as the character develops under the scrutiny of the interviewers. If the interview does not pick up momentum, it is usually because the questions are staying at the same level of generalization. ["How many people are in your family?" "How many friends do you have?" "What do you do for a living?"] Questions instead should be asked which relate to one another. ["Which person in your family do you like best?" "What kinds of things do the two of you do together?" "What's the farthest the two of you have ever biked together?"] Students are always quick to notice if the interview isn't getting anywhere and often have suggestions about what can improve it.

In order to sharpen listening skills and to keep the interview moving, ask students not to take notes during the questioning.

61

In this exercise we ask students to make a generalization based on the process of collecting, combining, subordinating, and emphasizing related pieces of information. This process is, of course, the same one required to formulate a thesis statement and a topic sentence, both of which contain a meaningful generalization.

"Student Biographies," page 10, is a good follow-up to this exercise because it reinforces and further develops the students' skills in questioning, listening, interpreting, and organizing.

SELF-PORTRAIT

PURPOSE AND DESCRIPTION

An exercise in gathering and organizing specific detail from which to develop a meaningful topic sentence. Students observe their own physical activities and thought processes, develop a topic sentence based on these observations, then write a short self-portrait. (The preceding exercise, "Collective Questioning," page 60, offers a good introduction to this exercise.)

LEVEL   Beginning.

CLASS PERIODS   One-quarter plus two.

ADVANCE PREPARATION   None.

ACTIVITY   Day One

Allow 10 minutes at the end of a class to ask students to keep track of their habits, tastes, and behavior over a period of one or two days. Tell them to watch themselves carefully and to make a list of everything that they can observe about themselves during that time. ["I curl my toes up when I'm sleepy," or "I never buy anything pink."] Their lists should contain at least 35 observations. Ask them to bring their lists of observations to class on an appointed day.

Day Two

On the day that students bring in their lists, ask them to see if their observations fall into any categories. Tell them to devise a scheme for labeling details that seem related in some way. For instance, they might put an "A" by the details which pertain to being alone and an "E" by those which include someone else, or they might divide their observations between approving ones and critical ones. Yet another way would be to divide their observations between physical activities and thought processes.

The students will not be able to fit all their details into categories but give them time to categorize as many of them as they can. This is the first step in organizing their material.

Next ask the students to select five to ten details on their lists which they have assigned to the same category. Ask each student to formulate a meaningful topic sentence about himself based on these five to ten details. Point out that the topic sentence will have to encompass all of the selected details and to suggest how those details are related. To be meaningful, the sentence also must include a point of view about the subject matter which suggests what details will follow. If the topic sentence fulfills all of these requirements, it will capture the reader's interest and make him want to continue reading. ["I only like talking when there's something to argue about," or "I will probably end up becoming President."] The details, selected for their common properties, should work together to support the topic sentence which introduces them.

Now ask each student to create a full paragraph by placing the topic sentence first and then developing it with the selected details. During class, ask everyone to write at least two paragraphs about himself using this method. For homework assign a third paragraph to be written in the same way. For each paragraph students may have to recategorize the details from their lists of observations.

Day Three

Have students exchange their paragraphs and read each other's work carefully, checking with the author if any words or phrases are illegible. Then ask volunteers to read another student's portrait out loud to the class without revealing the identity of the author. As each self-portrait is read, ask the students to see if the topic sentence comprehended its specifics, contained a point of view, and caught the readers' attention.

SPECIAL POINTS

For this exercise some students will write three fairly unrelated paragraphs while others may be able to generate a whole, unified essay. Depending upon the level of ability of your class, you might want to require that the three paragraphs be connected to each other and that the first topic sentence be a thesis statement for all of the following paragraphs.

We ask students to read each other's self-portraits to the class without revealing the writer for two reasons. One is that student writers are often able to hear their own work better when someone else reads it to them, especially if the material is personal, as a self-portrait is bound to be. The other reason is that when students do not know who the author of the self-portrait is, they are more likely to listen to it without preconceptions about the person and will be better critics of the actual writing. Often, the self-portraits reveal their authors to the listeners, but many will not. Of course, if any students want to acknowledge their own self-portraits during the discussion, they are free to do so.

"Self-Portrait" is similar to the next activity, "Portrait," except for its emphasis on the actual process of selecting related details from a body of undifferentiated observations in order to formulate the meaningful topic sentence.

PORTRAIT

PURPOSE AND DESCRIPTION

An exercise to learn how a topic sentence can be developed from a body of specific detail. A student chooses a person whom he knows, writes five details about him, uses his classmates to develop a thesis about the person, and then writes an essay developing this thesis. For beginning students this is a good introduction to the next activity, "One of the Family," page 68.

LEVEL   Beginning.

CLASS PERIODS   One.

ADVANCE PREPARATION   "Paragraphs in a Circle," page 73.

ACTIVITY

Ask each student to think of someone he knows well. Allow 10 to 15 minutes for each student to write five specific details about this person's character. ["Rob spends every spare moment after school alone in his barren back yard, practicing rope tricks."] Each of these statements should be developed fully, with vivid detail and carefully chosen verbs and adjectives.

When the specifics are listed, have the students exchange papers. At the bottom of the page, tell the student receiving the paper to write a generalization which covers all the specifics the first student listed. ["Rob is a loner," or "Being by himself is important to Rob."] The papers then should be returned to the original writer and shared with the class aloud.

Focus the group discussion on whether the generalization is supported by all of the details listed. The person who wrote the specifics should comment on the accuracy of the generalization and whether it truly applies to the person he has described. If the generalization is not accurate, the author should locate the misleading evidence in his group of five details. Perhaps he will need to add or subtract a detail to correct the misunderstanding about his subject's character.

Using either the generalization given him or his own generalization as his thesis and topic sentence, each student should write a descriptive essay about his chosen subject as homework. Each detail selected should further develop and support the thesis of the paper.

SPECIAL POINTS

This activity is good practice in careful, concise writing. Since no detail should be included in the paper unless it applies to the original thesis about the person, the student will have to use self-discipline in choosing the details. Usually a student will have information about his subject which is not relevant to the particular point he is developing, and he will have to suppress those facts in favor of relevant information. Be sure to make it clear to the students that the details should not focus on physical description but rather on character.

ONE OF THE FAMILY

PURPOSE AND DESCRIPTION

An exercise in using a point of view to develop a thesis statement supported by specific detail. Students write a biographical sketch of a family member (similar to "Collective Questioning," page 60, "Portrait," page 66, and "Self-Portrait," page 63).

LEVEL Any, especially good for beginning and intermediate.

CLASS PERIODS Three.

ADVANCE PREPARATION

Bring to class "Snoopy: The Authorized Biography of a Great American" by Charles Schulz, reprinted in "Introductions and Conclusions," page 51.

ACTIVITY Days One and Two

Ask students to define a *biographical sketch*. Together, arrive at a number of purposes for a biographical sketch. Be sure to include among those purposes: to give an overview of the events in someone's life, to give a brief insight into someone's life or personality, to describe someone's attitudes about his own life. You might also ask students to think of places where biographical sketches occur [book jackets, performance programs, letters of recommendation, informal descriptions of old friends to new friends or vice versa]. Point out that, in all of these cases, because the author of the biography has a definite point of view about his subject, he selects and organizes information in an attempt to convince readers to share his point of view about the subject.

Now read out loud to the students "Snoopy: The Authorized Biography of a Great American" by Charles Schulz, page 51. After you have finished, ask the students to identify the purpose of this sketch from among the number of purposes the class has already established for biographical sketches. Then reread the first sentence of the sketch to the class. Ask the students to identify the writer's point of view about his subject ("It is difficult to write an accurate biography of Snoopy . . ."), and any information which introduces readers to the subject, makes

68

them want to know more, and suggests what details will follow (". . . because many of his *recollections* seem to be *marred* by *fanciful dreams.*" Emphasis added.) Use this beginning sentence to explain what a meaningful thesis statement is: a statement which combines a point of view with a body of general information. Point out that a meaningful thesis statement must be broad enough to encompass a number of specific details, yet particular enough to capture the reader's interest.

Then tell the students that each of them is to write a biographical sketch about some member of his family. Ask students to choose as the subject for the sketch a family member they know well. Tell them to begin by locating a point of view toward the subject [affection, admiration, curiosity, irritation, tolerance].

Now ask the students to write a thesis statement, a statement which introduces the reader to the subject, makes the reader want to know more, suggests what details will follow, *and* conveys the writer's point of view about his subject. Remind the students that, in writing their thesis statements, word choice will convey point of view just as well as a direct statement. For instance, in the biography of Snoopy, the words "recollections," "marred," "fanciful" and "dreams" applied to a comic strip beagle suggest an ironic point of view on the part of the author.

While the students are composing their thesis statements, write on the chalkboard the following three headings for three separate lists: *Physical Details, Personality Traits, Life Experiences.*

When a number of students have completed their thesis statements, ask for a volunteer to read his statement out loud in order to demonstrate, with your help, how all the students should proceed with the next step of this assignment. Write the volunteer's thesis statement on the board above the three list headings.

Now ask the volunteer to supply up to ten physical details about his subject which support the thesis statement he has just read to the class. Write these details on the board under the first heading. Then ask him to supply a number of details about his subject's personality traits that would support the thesis statement. Also write these on the board under the appropriate heading. Lastly, ask him to describe any of his subject's experiences which would support the thesis statement. List these also on the board. Tell the other students that they should, at any time, ask the volunteer for an explanation if they do not understand how any one of the details he supplies supports his thesis statement.

69

If the students question one of the volunteer's details and if he cannot explain adequately how it supports his thesis statement, he may do one of two things: he may drop the detail from the list or, if he feels it is an essential detail about his subject, he may choose to modify his thesis statement in order to accommodate it.

When the volunteer has finished all three lists, ask the students to suggest ways the volunteer might organize these details in order to support his thesis statement most effectively. Tell the students that they are trying to determine an organizing principle for the sketch. Define *organizing principle* as a method of developing the point of view and information in the thesis statement so that the reader will react to the subject of the sketch in the same way that the writer does.

Now, using the three headings, have all of the students complete three similar lists of details for their own thesis statements. Tell them to leave out extraneous details, but to be ready to modify their thesis statements if they come up with new details about their subjects which seem essential to include.

For homework have students decide on an organizing principle for their lists of details and then write the biographical sketch. Remind the students that the sketch is not to be autobiographical, and that, although their points of view will shape their sketches, they are to focus on the subjects of their biographies, not on themselves. Specify the length of the sketches based on the ability level of the students.

Day Three

Have students read their sketches to the class. Be sure to cover four basic questions in the follow-up discussion:

1. What point of view was expressed by the thesis statement?

2. What details best supported the thesis statement?

3. Around which category was the sketch organized (physical detail, personality traits, life experiences, or a combination of two or three)?

4. What reaction did the writer lead you to have about his subject?

If you have a large class, you might arrange the students in smaller groups of six or eight to read and discuss their sketches. Before arranging these groups, however, have one student read his sketch to the entire class to establish a procedure for the discussions. You might even write the four basic follow-up questions on the board so the smaller groups will know how to proceed.

SPECIAL POINTS

It seems evident that people reach meaningful thesis statements only through an accumulation of specific, detailed information. Yet, in this exercise, we ask students to articulate a thesis statement about a subject before they list their store of details. Students should start by locating an *attitude* about someone in their family. Since their store of detailed information is likely to be vast, undifferentiated, and stretched over a period of many years, they can more easily isolate pertinent details after an attitude is established. This attitude, then, becomes the point of view expressed by the thesis statement and is the key to the students' selection and organization of supporting details.

When students are listing their supporting details, we encourage them to modify their thesis statements if they discover that the points of view they expressed in the thesis statements do not encompass the necessary details to develop the sketches as fully as possible. The constant testing of the thesis statements against the specifics and vice versa is an essential step in the writing process.

Once the students have completed their lists of details, they may organize them in a number of ways. A student who needs help with this might try focusing on the longest of the three lists of details he has written about his subject. For example, if a student has a particularly long list of details about his subject's personality traits, he might focus his sketch on those and use information from his list of physical details and life experiences to sharpen that focus. Whatever organizing principle a student chooses, it should develop the thesis statement in such a manner that the reader reacts to the subject of the sketch in the same way that the writer does.

We have deliberately not indicated where Day One ends and Day Two begins because this is determined by the pace of each individual class. If you have time during Day Two, you may wish to have students begin writing their biographical sketches in class.

Students usually enjoy this assignment because they have so much information available. However, for the student who has "nothing to say" about anyone in his family, you may wish to start him off by asking

71

some questions: "If you had to be trapped on a desert island for 10 years with someone in your family, whom would you choose? If you had to go shopping for clothes with a member of your family, whom would you take? Who are you least like in your family? If you had to be another member of your family, who would you be? If you could change a member of your family, whom would you alter and what changes would you make?

Some adolescents find it particularly difficult to write about their immediate families because they don't have enough distance from them or because their feelings are confused and inaccessible. Those students would do better to use someone removed from the immediate family as a subject for the biographical sketch. However, they should choose someone they know well and about whom they have a storehouse of detailed information.

Although the example of a biographical sketch you read to the class had a dog, Snoopy, for its subject, encourage the students to use human members of their families as subjects for their own sketches.

PARAGRAPHS IN A CIRCLE

PURPOSE AND DESCRIPTION

An exercise which demonstrates how a good topic sentence determines the organization and content of a paragraph. Each student writes a topic sentence and then passes the topic sentence to classmates who, one after another, add subsequent sentences to complete the paragraph.

LEVEL   Any.

CLASS PERIODS   One.

ADVANCE PREPARATION   None.

ACTIVITY

Review with the class what makes a good topic sentence. (See "Terrific Topic Sentences," page 101.)

Tell the students that the generalization and point of view expressed in a good topic sentence determine the content of the sentences which follow in the paragraph. All other ideas in the paragraph must be subordinate to the main idea in the topic sentence because each must illustrate the topic sentence's generalization and the author's point of view.

Arrange the class in a circle. If it is a large class, arrange the class in small circles of five students each.

Next, ask each student to begin a paragraph by writing a topic sentence, indented, at the top of a paper. Remind the students that the topic sentence should make a generalization about a subject and state an attitude toward that subject.

Now have each student pass his topic sentence to the student on his right. Ask each student to read the topic sentence which he has just received. Explain that now he is to add the second sentence of the paragraph. In order to do this, he must first locate the attitude in the topic sentence which needs to be developed and supported. Next, he must decide the best way to develop that attitude. There are three possible approaches: detailed description, anecdote, or exposition through fact and/or example. Often the topic sentence itself will provide a clue to which approach is best. Of course, some topic sentences will lend themselves to development through any of the three approaches. Tell the students that the second sentence must never be as general as the topic sentence; it must always deal with a more specific idea.

When you see that all of the students have added second sentences, ask them to pass the papers once again to the right. Have everyone do this at the same time. If you allow students to work at their own pace, a pile-up of papers at one student's desk can result.

At this point explain that each student is to add a third sentence to the two-sentence paragraph he just received. In adding the third sentence the student has less choice about what to write than for the second sentence. He must develop further what has come before him: the topic sentence with its attitude, and the second sentence which follows the topic sentence and begins to establish the type of paragraph (narrative, descriptive, expository). The third sentence must be at a still more specific level of generalization than the topic sentence and is usually even more specific than the second sentence, although it sometimes remains at the same level of generalization.

When you see that the students have added the third sentences to their paragraphs, again have them pass their papers to the people on their right. Each student is now to read the paragraph and add a fourth sentence which further develops the topic sentence and those which follow it. By the time students come to the fourth sentence, it should be clear that they have no choice but to continue the kind of detail which the second and third writers used to develop the main idea and the attitude toward it.

Once again have the students pass their papers to the right. Now ask the students to write a concluding sentence for the paragraph. The conclusion should be more general than the second, third, and fourth sentences, should refer to the topic sentence, and should possibly hint at a main idea which could be developed in a next paragraph.

Now have each student return the paragraph he has just concluded to the author of the topic sentence. Have each student read the paragraph which was generated from his topic sentence. Ask the student to mark in the margin any sentences which did not develop his topic sentence or which interrupted the movement from general idea to specifics.

Next, have a volunteer share his paragraph with the class by writing

74

it on the board. In class discussion, have the students examine that paragraph for the same kinds of inconsistencies which they looked for in their own paragraphs.

Now, using that same paragraph, have students look for the relationship among the sentences by asking them to articulate the subordination of ideas in the paragraph. / Do this by having the volunteer place slashes on the board at the end of each sentence to indicate that sentence's level of specificity in the following manner. // The most general sentence, the topic sentence, should be marked by one slash. /// The next sentence should be marked by two slashes to show that it develops and is subordinate to the topic sentence. /// The third sentence either functions on the same level as the second sentence and should be marked by two slashes, or it illustrates and is subordinate to the second sentence and should be marked by three slashes. /// The fourth sentence has two, three, or four slashes, and the concluding sentence will usually be at a level of two slashes. /// We have put slashes next to the sentences in this paragraph as an example of how this system works. //

Now have the students mark their own papers using the same method.

If there is time, ask for other volunteers to read their paragraphs aloud.

SPECIAL POINTS

As students write the topic sentences and the subsequent sentences, walk around the class helping them to make the transition from one sentence to the next. Often, you will be able to straighten out mistakes as students make them—pointing out how a new sentence misses the point and direction of the previous sentence(s).

In their ordinary writing, students rarely spend this amount of time working on the transition from one sentence to another and on the interrelationship of sentences in a paragraph. The device of passing the papers after each sentence helps students become conscious of the relationship of each sentence to the one before it and of how each sentence, though a discrete unit of meaning, must be clearly connected to all of the sentences in the paragraph.

You may be surprised that we recommend this exercise for advanced writers as well as for beginning and intermediate ones. We do this because we have found that many advanced writers have never taken the time to examine the structure of a paragraph in quite this way. Often they find this exercise illuminates what they knew intuitively.

PICTURES WITH A POINT

PURPOSE AND DESCRIPTION

An exercise in finding a theme and developing it by organizing and subordinating material relevant to the theme. Using randomly chosen photographs from magazines, a group of students looks for a central theme or idea in the photographs, organizes them to illustrate and develop the theme, and writes accompanying captions or text.

LEVEL   Beginning (especially for younger students).

CLASS PERIODS   Three.

ADVANCE PREPARATION

Several weeks before you give the assignment, ask the students to begin bringing in magazine pictures which have a message of some kind, are particularly beautiful, are pleasingly designed, and/or have emotional impact. Some suggested magazines are: *National Geographic, Saturday Evening Post, Time, Newsweek, Sports Illustrated, People,* any photography magazine. Each student should bring in about 10 pictures over the several weeks' time. Ask them to try to find at least one picture in each of the following categories: people, objects and still life, events and action, landscapes, animals, emotions, miscellaneous. Provide a shoebox in the classroom for each category. When students bring in pictures, ask them to sort the clippings into the appropriate boxes. If a student brings in a picture which fits into more than one category, ask him to put it in the relevant box which is less full.

Bring to class a large box of paper clips and one brown paper bag for each four students.

ACTIVITY   Day One

Divide the class into groups of four. Pass the seven boxes of pictures around the class and tell each group of students to select two pictures from each box. If you have a large collection of pictures, they can select four from each box. This should mean that each group of students will have at least 14 pictures. If there are more pictures available, each group can select up to 28 pictures. The more they have, the more alternatives there are for them to choose from in selecting a central theme for the assignment.

Now instruct the groups of students to examine the pictures carefully together, looking for and finally agreeing upon a common idea or theme which runs through most of the pictures. [The joys and sorrows of being alone.] When they have selected a theme, they are to set aside those pictures in their particular collection which are not pertinent to the theme they have chosen. The pictures they keep should be those which are relevant to and can support and develop the central theme upon which they have agreed.

Each group of students is now to order all the pictures they have kept in such a way that they develop their central idea. Tell them that they should organize the pictures just as they organize details in a paragraph, using one picture as a general statement and several pictures as subordinate to and supporting the general statement made by the main picture. Then they should move on to the next main picture. The students may see that they are now able to use some of the previously put-aside pictures to develop a subordinate aspect of their theme. At the end of class, ask the groups to stack the pictures in the tentative order which they have arrived at so far. Students should then clip the pictures together, put them in a paper bag, and mark the bag for easy identification. Keep the bag in the classroom overnight.

Day Two

Divide the class into the same groups as the previous day and ask them to finish arranging their pictures. Once the pictures are arranged in order, tell the groups to write an accompanying text. We suggest that the text take the form of captions appropriate for a story, for advertising copy, or for a short narrative.

When the text is written, ask the students to paper clip the text to the appropriate pictures so that the reader will know which part of the text goes with each picture. Store the pictures in the same way you did after Day One.

Day Three

Have students share the completed assignments with the class. If possible use of an opaque projector to permit the class to see the illustrations as the text is read. If an opaque projector is not available, have the class share their work in groups small enough so that everyone in the group can see the illustrations as the text is read.

In discussing the finished work, ask the students to evaluate the appropriateness of the text for the pictures and vice versa. They should also look for the way the larger theme in the work is developed by the use of subordinate ideas and details in the pictures.

SPECIAL POINTS

Satire is often an appropriate technique for students to use in this assignment. The pictures can be used to exaggerate or provide ironic contrast to the text. Repetition of the same picture can be used to emphasize an idea.

Keep the pictures gathered for this assignment to form a permanent collection. Ask the students to return them to their original boxes when the exercise is completed. You can use them many times—having each class add to the collection.

This is an excellent exercise for those students who have more highly developed visual sensitivity than verbal sensitivity. They see that selecting and organizing visual images is parallel in many ways to organizing written ideas. This same process of organizing and subordinating ideas which they used in arranging the pictures can be used in their written work.

This exercise is primarily for younger students and for students who need to be active. The fun of working with pictures and with other people keeps them involved.

The following variation on this assignment is suggested for those teachers and students who have access to filming and editing equipment and who have the expertise in editing necessary to put together a short 8mm film.

ADVANCE PREPARATION

Make, or ask a student to make, a short film with 15 to 20 separate shots arranged at random and consisting of disparate subjects; some small details; some larger, more general location shots; some action shots.

ACTIVITY

Show the film to the class. Show the film again and stop the action of the projector as necessary to allow each student to make a list of the shots in the film. Discuss what theme, message, or story could be inferred from the individual shots to serve as a unifying generalization. With the class, decide how to edit the film to illustrate and develop the agreed-upon theme. Together write dialogue or narration to make transitions easily between scenes. Edit the film, or have a student edit it, in the form agreed upon. Make a tape of the narration and synchronize it with the film.

TWO FLOWERS

PURPOSE AND DESCRIPTION

An exercise to develop students' abilities to analyze two similar objects through comparison and contrast. Students examine two flowers—one real, one plastic—and organize their observations about each. Next, they free associate using each flower as the basis of their associations. They then use all of this material in an essay comparing and contrasting the flowers.

LEVEL   Beginning and intermediate.

CLASS PERIODS   One.

ADVANCE PREPARATION

Plan to divide the class into groups of five. Bring enough plastic and real flowers to class so that each group of five students will have one of each type to examine.

ACTIVITY

Divide the class into groups of five. Hand out the flowers, one of each type to each group. Ask the students to examine the flowers carefully, to touch each with awareness of texture, to smell each, and to look closely at their colors and shapes.

Next, ask the students to divide a piece of paper lengthwise. Down the left side of the page ask them to write a list of descriptive details about one of the flowers. They should concentrate on sensory information [size, shape, color, smell, texture].

When this is complete, ask them to write a list down the right side of the page for the second flower. Each entry down the right side should be comparable to the entry on the same line on the left side of the page. For example:

REAL FLOWER   PLASTIC FLOWER

Deep red velvet color   Hard translucent fluorescent
                               pink

81

Then ask the students to take out a second sheet of paper. On this paper tell them they are to write two lists of associations, one for each flower. They must feel they have a reasonably complete list for the first flower before they begin the second list. Examples of entries on the associative lists:

REAL FLOWER:	PLASTIC FLOWER:
The feel of a chamois polishing cloth.	The barren smell of an empty school corridor.
The sharp perfume of a woman on the bus.	As lifeless as a styrofoam cup.

When the lists of associations are completed, have the students read all four lists to themselves and write a generalization about each flower. At this time, remind the students that the generalizations are to be used as a basis for comparing and contrasting the two flowers. The generalizations should be statements about a student's attitude underlying one set of lists for one flower that can be compared or contrasted to an attitude underlying the other set of lists for the other flower. You may wish to ask questions which will help your students identify these attitudes. [Is there one kind of feeling which appears often in these lists? Are there details which show opinions about the flowers or which show opinions about something the flowers remind you of? Are there particular kinds of sensory images that keep appearing in the lists—colors, shapes, textures, smells? Are these sensory images pleasant or unpleasant? Are there any places which the flowers bring to mind?] An example of the kind of generalization which might emerge is: "A dandelion is a flower of abandoned lots. A plastic rose is a flower of quiet rooms inhabited by lonely widows."

As homework have the students write essays comparing and/or contrasting the flowers. Using one of their generalizations as a thesis sentence, the students should write two or three paragraphs of description about the first flower—using its descriptive list and its associative list to support the thesis statement. Then, using the second generalization as a thesis sentence for the second half of the paper, the students should write two or three paragraphs about the second flower. Again the students will select material which supports the thesis statement. In this assignment their purpose is always to compare and contrast the two flowers. As they discuss the second flower, they should refer back constantly to the paragraphs about the first flower to make those comparisons and contrasts.

SPECIAL POINTS

This exercise is useful in strengthening students' analytical and descriptive abilities. They must draw on both to support their comparisons and contrasts.

This exercise also illustrates the richness and vitality associations lend to writing. The concrete observations from the first part of the exercise are one-dimensional and need the addition of the associations from the second part of the exercise to make the essay come alive.

When the students are working on the association part of this exercise, tell them that they will find many clichés in their responses, but that beyond these clichés lie their more original responses. Encourage them also to draw on personal memories and emotions. Tell the class to move beyond vague, general words [pretty, beautiful, sweet, ugly]—to provide details about the flower which will illustrate these qualities.

You may want to discuss the two major ways to organize comparison and contrast essays. The form described above is the sequential form, discussing one idea or object fully and then turning to a second idea or object—making comparisons and contrasts to the first one. The other major way is the parallel approach in which the writer moves back and forth from one object to the other either comparing or contrasting. He discusses a quality of the first idea or object; then moves to the comparable or contrasting quality of the second idea or object; then discusses a new quality of the first, and so on.

It will take the students one class period to get to the point where they can begin the essay which is to be completed as homework. Although this seems like a complicated and long exercise, it is much easier to do than to describe.

You can give more advanced students further practice in writing this kind of essay by asking them to contrast two objects, one contemporary and one old.

To facilitate such a comparison obtain two objects comparable in function, one contemporary and one clearly from an earlier era [an Indian arrowhead or knife and/or a modern arrow or knife; an old medicine bottle or milk bottle and new plastic bottle or paper milk carton; one of the earliest Coca-Cola ads and a modern Coke ad; an old beauty soap ad and a new beauty soap ad; a picture of an early luxury car and one of a contemporary luxury car; pictures or samples of older clothing and new clothing]. It is best to have the original objects in class, but pictures can be effective as well. If you have a large class, bring several pairs of objects.

Have the students organize their observations about these objects in the same way they did for the two flowers.

PLACE TO PLACE

PURPOSE AND DESCRIPTION

An exercise in comparison. Students observe people in two places which are different from each other but which also have many similarities. They then use these observations as the basis for a comparative essay.

LEVEL   Intermediate and advanced.

CLASS PERIODS   One-half plus one.

ADVANCE PREPARATION

Handout

PLACE TO PLACE

In this exercise you use your powers of observation in two locations which are quite different from each other but which have many similarities. In both places you watch people and take notes on their appearance and behavior. You also take notes on the appearance and atmosphere of each place. Then you organize your material and write a descriptive essay.

Choose one pair from the following list of places:

1. A museum and a department store
2. A hospital and a hotel
3. A church and a movie theater
4. A gas station and a fast food restaurant
5. A supermarket and a library
6. A health club and a car wash

OBSERVING ON THE SPOT

Spend one hour in each of the places you have chosen. In each place try to answer the following questions:

1. For what purposes do people come to this place?

2. Are there specific types of people who come here [people in particular economic groups, age groups, occupations, or related life styles]?

3. What are the functions of the people who work here?

4. What kinds of relationships do you see between the people who work here together, who come here together, and between those who work here and come here?

5. Do you interact with the people here? If so, how?

6. What evidence do you find of people enjoying themselves?

7. What evidence do you find of people having unpleasant experiences [indications of impatience, anger, irritation, nervousness, boredom]?

8. What is the physical appearance of this place?

9. How is the physical space organized?

10. What are the objects and areas which please or displease people here? What objects and areas please or displease you?

11. What is the mood of the place [chaotic, hushed, rushed, elegant]? What factors create this mood?

As you answer these questions, note specific details to illustrate any general observations you make: descriptions of particular people, bits of conversation, revealing anecdotes and vivid sensory data [colors, textures, sounds, and smells]. When you write your essay, these details will provide vitality and imagery which will enable your reader to experience what you experienced as you observed.

ACTIVITY   Day One

Provide 20 minutes at the *end* of a class for this part of the activity.

Distribute and discuss the duplicated handout questions. Ask the class to give some examples of the kinds of observations they might make in one place which could be compared with observations to be made in the other place. [The uniforms of the gas station attendants and the uniforms of the waiters and waitresses at McDonald's; the paging system of the hospital and the paging system at the hotel.]

Tell the students to set aside several hours to get to their places and to observe. It is best to give this assignment at least a week before it is due so that students will have a weekend in which to be on location and take notes.

Ask the students to bring their observations to class on the due date.

Day Two

On the day students bring their observations to class (at least a week after Day One), conduct a workshop to help them find themes for their essays and to assist them in ordering their observations under those themes.

First help them to look for an organizing principle or theme in their notes. Ask students to find material in their notes on the first place which can be compared with material in their notes on the second place [a description of a line of people at McDonald's which is comparable to a line of cars at a gas station]. Next ask the students to identify what most impressed them in the comparable material [particular people, an attitude, an atmosphere]. Then have students choose a theme for the essay based on the analysis they have just done. The theme should be a major idea which is applicable to each place and which can be developed by using many of the detailed observations. [The descriptions of the impatient lines of people at McDonald's and at the gas station could be used to illustrate a theme on the frantic pace of modern life.]

Now ask students to write a thesis sentence, based on this theme, to begin the essay and to shape the information which will follow. For example, "Whether you go to the County Museum of Art or to Grump's Department Store, you will find beautiful things under guard."

Next tell students to go over their notes and mark all those observations and details which will illustrate the theme stated in the thesis sentence. Finally have students organize the selected notes into outline form.

For homework, tell the students to write the essay based on their organized notes. Give them three alternative approaches to writing this essay: compare the two places observed by showing how the chosen theme is relevant to each place; or compare and contrast the two places by showing how each place does and does not relate to the theme; or, in an extended metaphor, use detail from the notes about one place to illustrate qualities about the other place.

SPECIAL POINTS

It is often difficult for students to organize the large amounts of material in this assignment into a coherent essay. For this reason we ask the students to begin organizing their notes in class where the teacher can help them as they struggle. A few well placed questions from the teacher can sometimes clarify a student's thoughts.

To help the students organize their essays, you may wish to distribute the handout on outlines, page 183.

If a student chooses to use an extended metaphor in this essay, it is important that he understand what one is. See "Essences," page 115, to help your class understand metaphors, and "People Landscapes" on page 118 to help them understand extended metaphors.

THESIS TIMES THREE

PURPOSE AND DESCRIPTION

An exercise to illustrate the differences among descriptive, narrative, and expository essays. To be given at the end of a semester's or year's study as a culminating exercise. Students formulate a thesis, then use the same thesis in the three different kinds of essays.

LEVEL   Advanced.

CLASS PERIODS   One-half plus two.

ADVANCE PREPARATION

The class should already have had experience writing descriptive ["Childhood Photos," "Place to Place," "Quick Study"], narrative ["Elementary, My Dear Watson," "The Egg," "Distortion"], and expository ["The Twin Problem," "The Language of Television," "A Cause"] essays.

ACTIVITY   Day One

Spend half of a class period reviewing with the class what constitutes a strong thesis and what makes an effective thesis sentence. (You may wish to refer to the discussion of thesis sentences in "Introductions and Conclusions," page 51.)

Now tell the class that they are going to write three essays. For all three essays they must use the same thesis, but one essay should be developed through description, one through narration, and one through exposition. Review with the class each approach. In a descriptive essay the main idea is developed primarily through use of detail; in a narrative essay the main idea is developed primarily through anecdote; and in an expository essay the main idea is developed primarily through argument and fact.

Now illustrate these approaches by showing how to develop one particular thesis in these three ways. Offer the class a sample thesis sentence such as, "Living in a large city can be lonely." Discuss how this thesis could be developed through description: descriptions of several lonely places in a city [a park, a crowded street, a bus depot, skid row], descriptions of lonely people in a city [an old person huddled on a bench in a subway station, a child in an empty schoolyard, a stout, middle-aged man snapping irritably at his dachshund]. Then discuss how the thesis could be developed through anecdote [a day in the life of an office worker, a ride on a bus, short encounters with a number of lonely people]. Lastly, discuss how the thesis could be developed through exposition [facts on the number of suicides in a city, quotes from sociologists about loneliness in urban areas, or psychological theories on the alienation of people who live under crowded conditions].

Point out that while the thesis must remain the same in each essay, the thesis sentence can either remain the same or change with each type of essay. The thesis can be stated explicitly through a thesis sentence or stated implicitly through the detail and point of view of the essay.

For homework, ask the students to develop a thesis on a subject about which they feel strongly. Tell them that because they will be using this thesis for their three fully developed essays, it should be completely clarified before they begin to write the essays. This entails developing a sharpened point of view and believing in the importance of what they are writing about.

Day Two

Use this second day as a workshop. Check the students' theses as they begin to write their essays in class. You may have to direct some students to refocus their main idea so that the thesis will be more suitable to use for the three types of essays.

Give the students at least a week before the assignment is due so that they will have time to write three carefully crafted essays.

Day Three

When the essays are completed, share several sets of them in class. Discuss the shifts in emphasis and effect created by the different approaches to the same thesis. Does the descriptive essay appeal particularly to the senses? How does the narrative essay engage the reader? How does the expository essay appeal to a sense of logic?

SPECIAL POINTS

In order to clarify the three different approaches to the essay, you may wish to refer to essays the students have already written using each approach.

This exercise is a good final assignment for a class. It allows students to test their abilities to deal with the major approaches to non-fiction writing. The areas of their strengths and weaknesses will be apparent in the differences among the three essays. Students will be able to see which of their essays developed the thesis most successfully and which approach they need to work on.

This exercise can also be used as a final take-home exam for a course in non-fiction writing.

3 TECHNIQUES OF STYLE

We begin this section with three exercises involving sentences: one focuses on structure and two on style. The next four exercises deal with ways to explore, maintain, and vary tone. Two exercises provide practice in using metaphor. The last two exercises examine the effect of point of view on style.

SENTENCE PATTERNS

PURPOSE AND DESCRIPTION

An exercise which shows how word order influences style. Students examine 12 sentence patterns. Then they write a paragraph describing a short, true incident—limiting themselves to one of these sentence patterns. Next they rewrite the paragraph using at least four patterns.

LEVEL   Any.

CLASS PERIODS   Two.

ADVANCE PREPARATION

Handout

SENTENCE PATTERNS

1. Begin with the subject.
   The sea is a whole world unto itself.

2. Begin with a prepositional phrase.
   In the past, the treasures of the sea were thought to be limitless.

3. Begin with an adverb.
   Slowly the sea reveals its secrets to us.

4. Begin with a gerund.
   Swimming in the Mediterranean is like bathing in a large turquoise tub.

5. Begin with an infinitive phrase.
   To protect our future on this earth we must protect ocean life as well.

6. Begin with a present participle phrase.
   Skimming the choppy surface, pelicans search hungrily for their evening meal.

7. Begin with a past participle phrase.
   Satisfied with the day's catch, the sun-parched fisherman turned his boat toward shore.

8. Begin with an adverbial clause.
   Whenever man sails away from his homeland, he is inevitably caught by the romance of the sea.

9. Use an appositive.
   The Pacific, the largest body of water on the planet, touches the shores of six continents.

10. Ask a question.
    Who wouldn't want to sail off to a tropical island?

11. Use an exclamation.
    Beware the fury of an Atlantic storm!

12. Use conversation.
    The captain warned, "All those with queasy stomachs should stay by the rail."

ACTIVITY   Day One

Distribute the handout to the class. Read and discuss each pattern. Write on the chalkboard a second sample sentence for each pattern which the class should develop together.

For homework ask the students to write one paragraph of at least six sentences on a topic from the following list:

A VIEW FROM A WINDOW   A STORM

MY CLOSET   AN INSECT

NIGHT SOUNDS

They must limit themselves to using only *one* sentence pattern in this paragraph. Pattern number one is probably the best one to choose because it is the most common, though students may select one of the others if they wish.

Day Two

Ask the students to rewrite their six-sentence paragraph in class. Require that they convey the same information as in the original paragraph, but this time they must use at least *four* different sentence patterns in the one paragraph.

When the paragraphs are rewritten, ask a few students to share both versions with the class. Discuss the implications of the differences between the two paragraphs. At this point it will become evident to the students that using a variety of sentence patterns influences the rhythm of a paragraph. The paragraphs composed of one pattern are monotonous; the paragraphs with a variety of patterns have more interesting rhythm and the sentences flow together more pleasingly. Also the emphasis in a sentence shifts with the use of a new pattern. [Some patterns emphasize movement; some emphasize time; some emphasize the subordination of one idea or action to another; others emphasize position.] The emphasis of a specific sentence becomes clear in context.

SPECIAL POINTS

Each student should learn to manipulate these sentence patterns. There are a variety of ways to achieve this. When you give any assignment, you might require that the students begin the paper with one particular pattern; or you might ask that each new paragraph start with a sentence differing in pattern from the opening sentence of the preceding paragraph. Alternatively, for a week or two have the students, as they enter the class, pick from a box slips of paper numbered from 1 to 12. Tell them to spend the first three or four minutes of class writing a sentence, in the pattern corresponding to the number they drew, on a topic which you have written on the board, or on a topic of their choice.

No matter what the level of your students, encourage them to practice these patterns so they can internalize them.

Remind students that they can also vary sentence structure by using simple sentences with compound subjects, verbs, or objects; compound sentences; complex sentences; or compound complex sentences.

For more advanced classes you will probably want to assign more than one paragraph for homework.

Encourage the students to use this list of sentence patterns when they revise any written work.

MORE VIVID SENTENCES

PURPOSE AND DESCRIPTION

An exercise in word choice and editing. Students are given a series of
sentences, and then a paragraph, which they are to alter by adding
expressive words or changing vague words to more specific ones.

LEVEL   Beginning and intermediate.

CLASS PERIODS   One.

ADVANCE PREPARATION

Handout

MORE VIVID SENTENCES

The following sentences are too vague: their nouns and verbs are general, and need modifiers (adjectives and adverbs). Alter these sentences
so that they provide a clear, specific picture for the reader. You may add
words and images, change words, and change sentence structure; or
you may eliminate the sentence because it is too abstract, and provide a
particular image in its place. Caution: Beware of overwriting. Make sure
your changes are meaningful and are there for a definite purpose.

EXAMPLE 1:

> *Before*   The room was noisy.
>
> *After*   From behind the heavy swinging door came
> the clattering crash of breakfast dishes.

EXAMPLE 2:

> *Before*   On the ground outside, my parents put some-
> thing down to sit on.
>
> *After*   On the rough, wet grass of the back yard my
> father and mother had spread quilts for us to
> sit on.

1. The park was an exciting place.

2. In the mirror he saw an unhappy face.

3. It was an old and ugly building.

4. I don't like doing household chores.

5. The boys who lived near him were always mean.

6. Switzerland is a beautiful country.

7. The big storm last year changed the way things looked at the lake.

8. Elise always spoke strangely when she spoke of her family.

9. Our neighbors fight a lot.

10. The beautiful spring day made her sad.

After you have rewritten the sentences, use the same techniques to make this paragraph more interesting:

I stayed in the house for the first time that night. The floor made a noise when I got into bed and so did the walls. It was a nice night but the wind blew outside. I hid in the bed and read a book. But I was not happy there. I kept thinking frightening thoughts and the noises were still there. I felt worse and worse as time passed.

ACTIVITY

Give the students the above handout to complete in class. Discuss possibilities for changing the first sentence; then have the class work independently. When the students have finished, ask for volunteers to read their changed paragraphs out loud. In class discussion help students see the importance of changing passive verbs into action verbs and replacing general statements with specific images.

For homework, ask students to find two paragraphs in their own descriptive writing (from past assignments written for class or from writing done on their own) which they feel lack vitality, are boring or too vague. The students should then rewrite these paragraphs using the same techniques they used to rewrite the duplicated exercise in class.

SPECIAL POINTS

Encourage students to use this technique for all papers they write.

TERRIFIC TOPIC SENTENCES

PURPOSE AND DESCRIPTION

An exercise to help students write focused, engaging topic sentences. Students study models of both poor and good topic sentences. On the basis of this analysis they then write poor and good topic sentences themselves.

LEVEL Beginning.

CLASS PERIODS One.

ADVANCE PREPARATION

Handout

TOPIC SENTENCES

TIRESOME TOPIC SENTENCES	TERRIFIC TOPIC SENTENCES
1. Many people in this country are overweight.	1. Obesity is so common in the U.S. that it has become our national disease.
2. Housework consists of many daily chores.	2. Cleaning up after a family of four can be a full-time job.
3. People come in all shapes and sizes.	3. If you want to see the human form in all its variety, go to Coney Island on a sweltering day in August.
4. Jane hates sports.	4. Jane is so uncomfortable on the playing field that she will do anything to get off it.
5. Vacations are a welcome relief from work.	5. Long sleepy vacation mornings erase memories of the jangling workday alarm clock.

6. If you want to relax, listen to music.

6. Loosen the collar; turn on the Bach: relax.

7. The existence of UFO's is always a controversial topic.

7. When Eric Ritter reported a flaming saucer-shaped object in the skies above his home in Tulsa, Oklahoma, local, state, and national authorities joined in discrediting his report.

8. Large modern cities depend on technology for their existence.

8. Imagine a city like Los Angeles without telephones, automobiles, or electric power.

9. Children who watch a lot of television are harmed by it.

9. A child saturated by six hours of situation comedy re-runs, cartoons and commercials, inevitably lapses into lethargy.

10. Things sure look different to people in love.

10. When my brother Billy fell in love, the whole family benefited from his gentler ways.

ACTIVITY

Distribute the handout to the class. Point out the function of a topic sentence—that it states the main idea of a paragraph. A successful topic sentence is not only a statement of fact but also includes an attitude or point of view about that fact. This attitude focuses the paragraph and shapes the selection of subsequent detail which will develop the main idea. A topic sentence which includes such an attitude makes a meaningful generalization. It is broad enough to encompass all the specific details in the paragraph to come, yet particular enough to capture the reader's interest.

With this in mind, examine the topic sentences on the handout with the class. Move from the "tiresome" sentence to the "terrific" one and compare the two. Look for words which convey the attitude or point of view. How specific are those words?

Then ask the class to choose one of the pairs of topic sentences and, as a group, to write a paragraph for each which develops the subject and attitude in the topic sentence. Write these paragraphs on the board. Now ask the students to compare the two paragraphs. Which paragraph is more interesting? Which paragraph is more specific? Which paragraph develops a clearer point of view? If the paragraphs have indeed developed their respective topic sentences, the students will see that the "terrific" topic sentence with its focused attitude produces a more effective paragraph.

Now ask the students to write their own topic sentences. They are to follow the handout format and write two lists. First have students write a "tiresome" topic sentence. Then ask them to rewrite that sentence into a "terrific" one by sharpening the attitude and making the generalization a meaningful one. Students should write and rewrite five topic sentences. These can be completed for homework.

SPECIAL POINTS

It may seem odd that we ask students to purposely write poor topic sentences in this exercise, but the process of composing poor sentences illuminates the steps necessary to transform them into good sentences. The contrast between the two sentences raises the students' level of awareness about what makes a topic sentence good. The process of changing their own sentences from poor ones to good ones is, of course, what we hope students will begin to do in all their writing.

THREE VOICES

PURPOSE AND DESCRIPTION

To enable students to isolate various voices in themselves and to understand how certain stylistic devices emerge naturally as the various voices speak. This is a teacher-directed short writing assignment which requires students to locate their angry, comforting, and persuasive voices.

LEVEL   Any.

CLASS PERIODS   One.

ADVANCE PREPARATION   None.

ACTIVITY

Direct students to think of a person, a thing, or an idea which makes them very angry. Don't allow students to write until they have definitely located a subject. Give the class a few minutes to do this. It helps some students to close their eyes to shut out distractions. Now give the students five minutes to write the angry things they want to say to or about that person, thing, or idea.

Next direct the students to visualize someone or something that needs comforting, something that is vulnerable or in distress. After a few minutes ask them to address that person or thing with the purpose of comforting it. Again give only five minutes for this writing.

Finally direct the students to visualize someone whom they want to persuade to do or to believe something. After a few minutes ask them to write to that person in the most persuasive way they know, attempting to win that person over to their own point of view. Allow five minutes for this writing also.

At the end of the writing part of this exercise tell the students they are going to find out which stylistic devices they have used in their three voices. Tell them that when they write with strong purpose they automatically employ certain stylistic devices, and that even though they may not know the names for them, the devices will nevertheless emerge as their papers are read. Ask for some volunteers to read at least two out of their three voices to the class.

As students discuss what makes a voice angry, comforting, or persuasive, list on the chalkboard the names for the various devices that they describe informally. Your list might include: metaphor; loaded language; repetition; abrupt sentence patterns; rhythm; elongated sentence patterns; onomatopoeia; parallelisms; active, passive, or imperative voices.

Help them to see that certain voices use characteristic devices. Often the angry voice will use loaded language, speak in abrupt sentences, and relentlessly repeat key words or phrases. The comforting voice may soothe with long rhythmical sentences, linked together by conjunctions and uninterrupted by punctuation. The persuasive voice may avail itself of logical, parallel sentence patterns and strong, active or imperative verbs. Ask the students to listen for distinct differences among the voices, and to describe what it is that creates the differences. Also ask them to compare the different devices various students used to express similar sentiments and ideas.

SPECIAL POINTS

To cover as many voices as possible in class discussion, comment on only the most striking devices any one individual employed. Too much attention paid to a single paper takes the energy out of the discussion of the other papers.

It is important for students to see that when they are writing sincerely, with their own voices, they have a wealth of stylistic devices to draw from. This exercise allows students to experience those devices rather than to simply execute them. Since you will identify in class discussion only those devices that were employed by the students themselves, each device will already belong to at least one of the students. In this way, students will understand stylistic devices not as formal and unfamiliar creatures, but as natural consequences of a writer's voice.

Even though students may ask for an example of an angry, comforting, or persuasive voice at the beginning of this assignment, it is better to insist that they find their own. An example from you might set the tone for the whole class and hinder students from locating their individual voices.

105

Since this exercise is simply a demonstration of how voices work, there can be no formal evaluation of the students' papers. Some students will feel too personally exposed to read any of their voices and their privacy should be respected. It is important to collect these papers, however, and to comment on them in writing in the same way that the group collectively commented on those that were shared.

A ROUND

PURPOSE AND DESCRIPTION

To heighten students' understanding of and sensitivity to tone. Three students work in shifts to create a unified piece of writing.

LEVEL Intermediate and advanced.

CLASS PERIODS Two or three.

ADVANCE PREPARATION

"Sentence Patterns," page 95. (It will help if "Sentence Patterns" immediately precedes this exercise.)

ACTIVITY Day One

Ask each student to write one sentence on a piece of scratch paper. At random choose five volunteers to copy their completed sentences on a portion of the chalkboard. When they are finished, on another portion of the board list the five elements that set and maintain tone: word choice, sentence patterns, quantity and quality of detail, level of abstraction, point of view.

Using the five student sentences for examples, point out to the class how word choices and sentence patterns help set tone. Show the students that sentences with similar quantity and quality of detail have similar tone. Also show them that sentences which express similar levels of thought, from concrete to abstract, have similar tone as well. Finally, help them to recognize points of view in the sentences by asking them to identify any attitudes the writers expressed through their sentences. Emphasize that similar points of view often set similar tones.

When the students are familiar with the five elements and have agreed on a working definition of tone and how it is achieved, have the class divide into groups of three. Ask each student to write an introductory paragraph to an essay about a short, true personal experience. Tell the students they will have ten minutes to do this.

At the end of ten minutes have students pass their papers to the person on the right. Tell the students to read the introductory paragraphs they have just received and to consult with the original writers concerning any questions of legibility. They may not ask any other kinds of questions. Then, in the margin of this paper, have each student write down the five elements of tone.

Tell the class that, for homework, they are to write a middle section of one or more paragraphs to follow the introductory paragraphs they just received. This middle section should be written in a tone as similar to the original paragraph as possible. Remind students to refer to the list of five elements when determining the tone of the introductory paragraph. They should also pay attention to any hints in the first paragraph about what the original writer would have said next. Although students will be making up the middle section, they should be careful to make it a believable continuation of whatever introductory paragraph they have received.

Day Two

Have students arrange themselves in exactly the same combination of three people as they did on the previous day. Have each student pass the paper worked on for homework to the one person in the group who has not yet contributed to it. Give the students a few minutes to read these papers and to consult the writers of the other two sections with regard to any questions of legibility. Now ask students to write a concluding paragraph for the paper they have just received, again paying close attention to the tone and subject matter of the previous paragraphs. If students feel there are discrepancies in tone between the introductory and middle paragraphs of the papers they have received, tell them to refer back to the tone of the introductory paragraph as a model for their conclusions. Tell them they have twenty minutes to conclude these essays.

At the end of twenty minutes have students return the papers to the authors of the introductory paragraphs. List the five elements of tone once again on the chalkboard. Now ask students to consider the tone of their own introductory paragraphs. Have them pick out and underline places where later writers took the first author's word choice, details, and attitudes into account. Instruct them to double underline words or phrases that don't seem consistent with the general flow of their original paragraph.

After students have had a chance to evaluate the pieces they began, have a few students read their papers out loud to the entire class. Have the students engage in a similar evaluation of these papers. If you have a very large class, you may wish to divide the students into smaller groups for this discussion after they have talked about one or two papers as a whole class.

SPECIAL POINTS

Have students begin the essays by describing a true personal experience because that gives their introductions a body of remembered detail, a real direction, and an already developed point of view. The introductions, therefore, are usually substantial enough to provide subsequent writers with adequate hints about what really happened. Since the introductions describe an actual event, they also establish a fairly accessible tone as well.

Stress during discussion that the function of the middle and concluding writers was not to guess what the original writer's real experience was; instead it was to maintain the first author's tone and follow up believably what he began.

Usually students are sensitive to how the contributions of the two later writers altered or developed their own introductions, so the underlining process is a natural step in this exercise. You may want to ask more advanced students to list in the margin, beside their underlining, which of the five elements contributed to consistency or discrepancy of tone between the introductory paragraph and later ones.

Since each essay has three writers, the students have a broader investment in the class sharing. They are quick to pick up irregularities of tone unless the essays have no continuity whatsoever.

We have used this exercise as a way for students to practice analyzing and controlling tone. Depending on the level of understanding and skill of the students, the discussion of this exercise can be limited to pointing out one useful technique for setting tone, such as similarity of sentence patterns; or discussion can be expanded to demonstrate many interdependent techniques for setting and maintaining tone.

109

This exercise provides some very particular devices which weaker students can turn to—perhaps with your help—if they find it difficult to continue the tone of the previous paragraph. Through this process, such students often learn for the first time how they can control the elements of tone.

We suggest that the next exercise, "Lies," is an effective activity to use either just before or just after this one.

LIES

PURPOSE AND DESCRIPTION

To increase students' sensitivity to tone in others' writing and to help them develop consistency of tone in their own writing. Students write three paragraphs, each describing a different event in the writer's life: two of these events are true; one of them is false. The class then tries to pick out their classmates' false paragraphs.

LEVEL Any.

CLASS PERIODS Two.

ADVANCE PREPARATION None.

ACTIVITY **Day One**

Ask students to recall any interesting experiences they had either recently or in the past which they remember vividly. Ask them to recapture, in one paragraph each, whatever was interesting about two of the experiences. In both paragraphs they are to be absolutely *honest*— neither adding, deleting, or changing any detail from what they remember. Also ask them to write a third paragraph. This one is to be a description of an imaginary experience and is to be absolutely *false*. In this paragraph they should be careful that each detail be deliberately not true. They may not use any half-truths; but, rather, must invent every part of the experience. Nevertheless, this paragraph is to be written in a manner consistent enough with the other two so that it would not be obvious to a reader which of the three was false. Tell students to be careful not to reveal, either by title or by the order in which they are written, which of their paragraphs is false. Emphasize that their writing should be as legible as possible.

Day Two

Collect the completed papers and pass them out at random. Let each student read to himself the three paragraphs he has just been given and clarify anything about which he is not certain with the author. Now ask for a volunteer to read one of the papers out loud. When all three paragraphs are read, ask the listeners to vote by a show of hands for the one they think is false. After the vote ask students to explain what made them vote the way they did.

Which clues are most reliable in distinguishing the false from the true? Is the physical detail impoverished or exaggerated in the imaginary paragraphs? Does a more defined attitude come out in the false or true paragraphs? How did the balance between specific details and generalizations in the true paragraphs compare with the false one? Only after these explanations are complete should the writer reveal which paragraph was false. There is usually time to share four or five of these papers in one class period.

SPECIAL POINTS

This exercise helps students distinguish between the language of experience and that of imagination through both writing and listening. They enjoy the challenge of creating an imaginary experience in such a way that others will believe it, and they equally enjoy trying to pinpoint which of their class members' experiences aren't true. It is important that the paragraphs be read by someone other than the author so that the clues to the false paragraphs come strictly from the writing and not from preconceptions students may have about each other or from give-away gestures and expressions.

Students almost always identify the false paragraphs. We have found that the biggest clue is a disparity they note in the level of generalization between the false and true paragraphs.

Students enjoy listening to these paragraphs and it may take more than one class period to read enough of them. After the discussion of the papers, students will probably want to discuss the difference between the ways they went about writing their true paragraphs and the ways they went about writing the false ones.

TWO TONES

PURPOSE AND DESCRIPTION

To practice controlling tone, students write about one neutral object from two different points of view.

LEVEL   Any.

CLASS PERIODS   One or two.

ADVANCE PREPARATION

Students should either have done the exercise "A Round," page 107, or else be familiar with the elements which make up tone.

Bring to class several brief examples of different types of tone in writing.

ACTIVITY

Ask the class to think of as many different types of tone as possible. Record each of them on the chalkboard [pompously solemn, condescending, relaxed and informal, coldly formal, sad, sarcastic, inspirational, critical, angry, enthusiastic, naive, analytical].

Then read one of your examples to the class and ask the students to identify the tone. Next ask the students to list out loud as many elements as they can from the example which combine to create that tone. Be sure that they touch on word choice, sentence patterns, quantity and quality of detail, level of abstraction, and point of view. Repeat this group process once or twice with examples of different types of tone.

Afterwards, in class discussion, have the students practice different tones by changing their points of view about the same situation. Ask students to imagine being on a bus and crowded by another person. What words and tone would they use to protect their physical space: if they were a tall person and the bus were full of little children? if they were a little child in a bus filled with tall adults? if they were in a bus entirely filled with good friends?

Then list the following objects on the chalkboard: a TV set, a slice of chocolate cake, a cap pistol, an automobile, a dictionary, a jack-hammer,

113

a trumpet, a swimming pool, a broom, a piece of paper. Ask students to describe in writing one of the subjects on the list, using two very different tones chosen from the list of tones on the board. Tell students to write a description at least two paragraphs long using the first tone and a description of at least two paragraphs using the second tone. They should write the name of the tone they have used at the bottom of each description. To do this assignment, students may want to think of a person whose point of view could be expressed by the tone they have picked [naive—a young child; critical—a parent] and then try to write the way they think that person would write. Tell the students that if they find writing in a chosen tone particularly difficult they should select a different tone. Some tones will not accommodate describing an object as well as others will.

After the students have finished, ask volunteers to read both descriptions to the class without naming the tones they used. Ask the rest of the students to try to identify each tone and say why they believe that was the tone intended by the author. As they listen, students should jot down or remember specific words or phrases of the author's which have particular color and seem to reveal a point of view. They should cite these words or phrases as proof of the tone they assign to the author's paper.

SPECIAL POINTS

This exercise illuminates how tone colors description of neutral objects. If you wish, this exercise can be a good transition to a discussion of propaganda (see "Introduction to Propaganda," page 167).

ESSENCES

PURPOSE AND DESCRIPTION

A classroom game which enlarges students' ability to understand and use metaphor. A member of the class thinks of a well-known person. The rest of the class then tries to discover the identity of that person by asking questions which require a metaphoric response. [What machine is this person? What animal is this person?]

LEVEL   Beginning.

CLASS PERIODS   One.

ADVANCE PREPARATION   None.

ACTIVITY

Ask one student to think of someone everyone in the class is sure to know. It might be a famous person or even someone in the classroom. However, you may want to specify that the mystery person be someone outside of the class to avoid the possibility of students using the game to tease each other. Tell the other students it is their task to guess who this mystery person is. The class may ask questions of the student, but they must do so only by requesting a comparison. [If this person were an animal, what would it be? If this person were a fruit, what would it be?] Have another student go to the chalkboard and write down the essentials of the responses so that students can piece together the information as they go [animal—doe, fruit—persimmon]. Double or qualified answers may be given, such as, "a cross between a raccoon and a deer." Remind the student who is making the comparisons to answer thoughtfully, being as accurate about the qualities of the mystery person as possible.

Make sure the students understand the distinction between comparisons and possessions. Sometimes students misunderstand the nature of the comparative process and respond with descriptions of what the mystery person actually possesses rather than what he or she reminds them of. Such a misunderstanding will lead a student to answer the question, "If this person were a car, what kind would he be?" by telling the actual kind of car the person really owns.

After at least 20 students have asked questions, allow the student who gave the answers to modify or change any responses which have been recorded on the chalkboard. If the student feels all of the recorded responses are correct, the rest of the class may now try to guess who the mystery person is. The first person to guess successfully gets to think of the next mystery person, and the game continues.

If no one guesses correctly, ask the student who was being questioned to reveal the mystery person. Some discussion may follow as to the accuracy of some of the responses. After this discussion, have this student choose someone else to think of a mystery person and to respond to the class's questions.

An average class period provides time for about three rounds.

After the exercise is over, ask students if it seemed at all familiar to them to think of a person in terms of seemingly unrelated objects or ideas. Often they admit that they make these kinds of associations mentally but don't quite know how to verbalize them. Urge them to practice using associations in their descriptive writing. Point out that the ability to make associations which dip below the surface and touch on essences gives life and originality to their writing.

SPECIAL POINTS

This exercise is especially helpful to the student who is intimidated by the formal concepts of metaphor or simile and who believes he does not see the world in such terms. It is often just this student who will make the correct guess based on the assorted comparisons.

It is best to make sure that the first student to be questioned is someone who will not be uncomfortable with the process and will enjoy making the comparisons. After a few rounds, students often come up with unique categories for their questions. [If this person were a period in history, what would it be?]

You may want to encourage students to play Essences in small groups on their own.

116

PEOPLE LANDSCAPES

PURPOSE AND DESCRIPTION

To help students experience the descriptive power of metaphor. An exercise in extended metaphor, best used with a class which has been working together long enough so that the students are familiar with each other's appearances and personalities. In this exercise students transform each other into landscapes.

LEVEL   Intermediate and advanced.

CLASS PERIODS   Two.

ADVANCE PREPARATION   None.

ACTIVITY   Day One

Tell your students that each of them is going to create a landscape by using another student in the class as a model. Ask students to silently choose one person in the room to become the model for their landscape. Tell the students that, without revealing their choices, they are to think carefully about their models. How would they describe their model's personality [light, airy, stormy, unpredictable]? What colors and textures do they associate with their models? What kinds of shapes [angular, spherical, elongated]?

Tell the students that each completed landscape should include descriptions of the colors, textures, topography, geography, weather, flora, and fauna which best represent the way the writer sees the model. For instance, a particularly unpredictable person who quickly shifts from one mood to another might, as a landscape model, inspire the writer to create a day of sun and rain over a turbulent ocean. Tell the students that although they may base their descriptions of their models on landscapes with which they are familiar, they may have to invent non-existent landscapes (or parts of landscapes) to capture adequately the combination of physical and/or personality traits they observe in their models. Make sure the students understand that they are not to describe their models literally; instead they are to describe them metaphorically.

117

Suggest that they jot down some immediate analogies to or descriptions of their models before they begin writing the actual landscapes [eyes like puddles; a voice as sharp as the February wind off Lake Michigan]. Allow an entire class period for thoughtful writing. For homework, have students complete the landscapes.

Day Two

Have students read their landscapes out loud to each other. Ask the class to observe what characteristics in the model the author emphasized in the landscape: physical features, personality traits, movements, gestures, idiosyncracies. Ask the class to discuss how the writer's feelings toward the model were expressed. If the writer was fairly sensitive to the qualities of the model, there will usually be a consensus about which student was the subject. If there is a lot of disagreement, a discussion usually follows as to why.

SPECIAL POINTS

In comparing a person to a landscape the students will have created an extended metaphor. That is, they will have explained one thing at length in terms of another. Each piece of the landscape should be associated with some observation or feeling they have about their models. And through a combination of feeling and observation their metaphors will express an abstraction which they may not have been able to express directly. For this reason students usually enjoy hearing each others' landscapes. They like to guess who inspired what.

Students can evaluate the accuracy of their metaphors by the number of other students who can identify the intended model. They also see that a deliberate, thoughtful metaphor provokes discussion, while metaphors which are too obvious or too obscure usually don't inspire much conversation. Leave enough time for follow-up discussion.

The effectiveness of "People Landscapes" depends upon your students' abilities to use each other thoughtfully as models. If the students have hostile feelings towards each other, they won't be able to do this.

If you have students who aren't familiar with one another, we suggest that you precede this exercise with "Student Biographies," page 10. Have students use the subject of these biographies as the model for the landscape. In this way, each student will be sure to have a body of information to draw on when creating the landscape.

118

AUDIENCES

The following three exercises are interdependent and should be done in sequence. The entire assignment requires three to four class days to complete.

PART I

PURPOSE AND DESCRIPTION

To show students how point of view and intended audience shape writing style. Students examine articles published in various contemporary magazines.

LEVEL   Intermediate and advanced.

CLASS PERIODS   One.

ADVANCE PREPARATION

1. Find a short article of general interest in a recent issue of a popular magazine. Duplicate the first and last paragraph of the article for a handout.

2. Duplicate the body of the article on a separate handout.

3. Bring to class a number of recent issues of different kinds of magazines: *Harpers, Seventeen, Newsweek, Ladies' Home Journal, New Republic, MS., Reader's Digest.* If possible find some magazines which have articles about topics similar to the one you duplicated to hand out to the students.

Handout
_____

HOMEWORK—AUDIENCES

Find a magazine that interests you. Choose three articles from that magazine to read and to analyze. For each of your articles follow the same procedure we used when we analyzed the two articles in class.

Part I

First look at only the beginning and ending paragraphs. Note in the margin of the paragraphs any stylistic techniques you observe [simplicity or complexity of language, metaphors, similes, loaded language, sentence patterns, emphasis]. Based on those observations, answer the following questions on a separate sheet of paper:

1. To whom is the author speaking [consumers, teenagers, business executives]?

2. What kind of person would probably not care to read the article?

3. How can you identify the opinions of the author?

4. What do you expect to find in the body of the article?

Part II

Now read the body of the article. Make notes to yourself in the margin concerning word choice patterns, sentence complexity, implicit or explicit judgments, emphasis, and any other techniques that seem to identify each article's intended audience and point of view. Based on the techniques you noted, answer the following questions about each article. Write your answers on the same paper you used to answer the questions in Part I.

Concerning the audience:

1. Was the article aimed at a specific social or economic group [people who travel, homeowners, people on a tight budget]?

2. Did the author make *any* assumptions about the lifestyle of the intended audience [singles, partygoers, outdoorsmen]?

3. What degree of familiarity does the author assume the reader possesses about the subject?

Concerning the author's point of view:

1. How does the author feel about his subject?

2. What response does the author intend to evoke from the reader [anger, empathy, interest, amusement, belief, disbelief]?

Bring your magazine and your answers to the questions to the next class meeting.

120

To this same class meeting bring a newspaper article about something which sincerely interests you.

ACTIVITY

Hand out the first and last paragraphs of the article you duplicated for the class. Have the class read the paragraphs. Without distributing the homework handout to the students, use the questions from Part I on that handout to lead a discussion about the stylistic techniques that students observe in these two paragraphs.

At the end of this discussion, hand out the body of the article. Again without distributing the homework handout, use the questions from Part II of that handout to lead a discussion about the connection between stylistic techniques, intended audience, and point of view in the entire article.

If time permits, read a second article to the class. Select this article from a different magazine than the one from which you took the first article. Try to find an article which is similar in subject matter but different in intended audience and point of view. Follow the same procedure for reading and analyzing this second article as you did for the first one.

Distribute the homework handout. Discuss briefly with the class the variety of magazines from which they may choose to do the homework assignment. Some students may need to borrow one of the magazines you brought to class if they don't have a selection at home.

SPECIAL POINTS

In selecting the two magazines from which students read and analyze articles in class, we've found it most useful to select two magazines directed toward two different audiences interested in generally similar subjects [*Good Housekeeping* and *Vogue*, or *People* and *Newsweek*]. Such a selection will provide articles with similar subject matter as a basis for comparison. At the same time the varying intended audiences and points of view of the articles will provide examples of contrasting writing styles.

121

We start out by having students examine only the first and last paragraphs of any article because that provides students with a finite and therefore accessible amount of writing to begin analyzing. The first paragraph of a well-written article will reveal its intended audience, and the last paragraph will usually emphasize the author's most encompassing point of view. Furthermore, a close and thoughtful look at the beginning and ending paragraphs helps students learn how to focus more deliberately on the body of the article.

We don't give the students the homework handout until they have completed their analysis of one or two articles in class because the questions about stylistic techniques, intended audiences, and point of view should come first from you. Students often feel condescended to when they are asked to respond to a list of printed questions. Nevertheless, the questions must be asked; and if they come first from you, they will seem more immediate, relevant, and challenging. We pass the questions out for the homework assignment because the students will need them to do a thorough analysis of their articles.

AUDIENCES—PART II

PURPOSE AND DESCRIPTION

To exercise the skills involved in writing for an intended audience. Students list the basic information contained in a newspaper article; then write an article title for that body of information in the style of the magazine they have analyzed previously. At home, they write an article to follow that title, again in the style of the previously analyzed magazine. This is the second part of an interdependent three-part exercise.

LEVEL   Intermediate and advanced.

CLASS PERIODS   One (or two, see SPECIAL POINTS).

ADVANCE PREPARATION   Audiences—Part I.

ACTIVITY

Review briefly the way information is developed in a newspaper story (see "News Story," page 152). Then ask students to list the information

122

in their newspaper articles in the same sequence as the article presents it. Tell students to include in the list all the basic information in the article. If their articles are well written, students will find that every sentence gives basic information which will make some new contribution to their lists.

After students have finished the listing, ask them to rewrite a title for the newspaper article in the style of the magazine they analyzed for homework. Remind students to consider carefully word choice and sentence structure as well as intended audience. To help them do this, they will need to refer to the answers they wrote to the questions on the handout "Homework—Audiences," concerning the three articles they analyzed. This exercise is the students' first attempt at interpretation through imitation, and some students will need your added support and direction during this phase of it. To be sure that each student understands adequately Part II of the assignment, have students read their rewritten titles to the class to see if other students can identify the type of audience for which the article is intended.

Have students use the titles they rewrote in class as the starting point for their homework assignment. They are to rewrite their entire newspaper articles to suit the tastes, interests, and style of the magazine they analyzed for homework the night before. The rewritten article, like the rewritten title, should be geared to catch the interest of the magazine's intended audience. Again, to help them do this, students will need to refer to their answers to the questions on the handout "Homework—Audiences."

Depending upon the kind of audience students choose and the kind of magazine they rewrite the article for, they may find that they need more information than the newspaper account contained in order to accommodate the style of their chosen magazine. In this case, and only when they have exhausted the factual information from the newspaper article, they may invent extra details which seem reasonable and which need to be included in order to re-create the magazine's style.

When the assignment is completed, require that the students' original newspaper article, the list of information from it, their answers to the questions on the handout "Homework—Audiences," and the invented magazine article be turned in together. The list from the newspaper helps students identify basic information and helps you to see how they used that information in their magazine articles.

123

SPECIAL POINTS

This is a sophisticated exercise in imitation. Depending upon the level of competence of your class and on their ability to work independently, you may want to use the entire homework assignment as a second day's class activity instead. We have found it useful for some students to try this assignment on their own first, to locate their particular difficulties and questions about it. Others are more comfortable having a teacher available as an immediate resource when difficulties arise.

AUDIENCES—PART III

PURPOSE AND DESCRIPTION

To reinforce newly learned skills of analysis and imitation with an emphasis on students' ability to use them independently. Students, on their own, rewrite a newspaper article in the style of a second magazine chosen to contrast with the first magazine they imitated in "Audiences—Part II." This is Part III of an interdependent three-part exercise.

LEVEL Intermediate and advanced.

CLASS PERIODS One.

ADVANCE PREPARATION Audiences—Parts I and II.

ACTIVITY

Have students share their rewritten articles from the "Audiences—Part II" assignment with the class. In the ensuing discussion, determine intended audiences and authors' points of view by noting word choice, sentence patterns, organization of material, and selection and emphasis of detail. If two students chose to write for the same magazine, take this opportunity to compare the styles of their articles.

After sharing these rewritten articles, if the students seem to understand what writing for an intended audience entails, ask them to write an article for a second, very different magazine of their choice. Require that the students go back to the original newspaper article which provided the information for the second article. (To use the first rewritten magazine article as a model for the second would be confusing and misleading.) This time the assignment is to be done entirely as homework, the title included. Suggest that students choose a magazine with a writing style in obvious contrast to the style of the magazine previously imitated. Magazine combinations such as *Newsweek* and the *National Enquirer, MS.* and *Ladies' Home Journal, Esquire* and *Seventeen* stand in good stylistic opposition to one another.

SPECIAL POINTS

Students may choose to organize their articles for the second magazine in a way entirely different from the first rewritten article. They will probably need to shift emphasis, weighting some details more and some less than they weighted them for their first articles. They may want to change the order of the details as well, since order will affect what gets emphasized. Of course they will have to pay particular attention to their choice of language for these second articles.

In the writing of the second article, students get a sense of their ability to shape and present information to reach two different audiences. If you choose to have students share these second articles in class, give each writer a chance to explain some of the stylistic choices he made in order to reach the new audience.

This series of assignments helps students see the connection between writing style and intended audience. When students finish the series, they will have practiced analyzing and imitating style with the purpose of identifying and writing for a particular audience. As they gain a sense of how to reach various audiences by the use of various styles, they inevitably find that their writing has greater range and impact.

Another series, similar to this one, which exposes students to contemporary newspaper writing, is "From the Newspaper," page 144. See also "Distortion," page 163.

THE LANGUAGE OF TELEVISION

PURPOSE AND DESCRIPTION

To develop analytical skills and awareness of attitudes reflected in word choice. To practice developing a thesis based on a large body of observed detail. Students analyze the language used in six half-hour television programs. They then write a paper with a thesis stating an attitude reflected in the programs and with evidence made up of the language used on the programs.

LEVEL   Intermediate and advanced.

CLASS PERIODS   One-quarter plus one.

ADVANCE PREPARATION   None.

ACTIVITY   Day One

Near the end of a class period, tell your students that as homework for the next two or three days they are to watch and listen carefully to six half-hour television programs. These programs must all be of the same type [game shows, soap operas, children's programs, newscasts]. For the first half hour they are only to listen and watch. Then, for the next five half hours they are to list those words and phrases which seem to predominate in the programs they have selected, and which seem to characterize the attitudes of the people on the programs who use them. Tell students to pay particular attention to words of approval or disapproval and words that express feelings. What are the connotative implications of these words? [What words are used to mean good: "excellent," "far-out," "groovy," "exemplary," "fantastic," "swell"? What phrases express sadness, anger, frustration, or anxiety? What is implied if a woman is repeatedly addressed as "broad," "chick," or "baby"?] Professional or technical terminology should *not* be on this list.

Day Two

In class, after students have watched all six programs, have them look over the words and phrases they listed to see if they can determine the underlying attitudes of the people who used them. They can do this by

126

asking questions about the implications of the words chosen. [If the game show host describes each correct answer as "stupendous," what does this reveal about his attitude toward the game?] Did students start off with their own preconceived attitudes about the programs they were to watch? What kind of repetition became apparent in their lists? How explicit was the language on their lists? How abstract or concrete? Were clichés used? Metaphors and/or similes? Emphasize that the students' speculations must be based on the repeated use of words or phrases. They should ask themselves, why are these words or phrases repeated? What do they have in common? What attitudes do they seem to reflect?

After the students have come up with a number of questions and answers concerning the implications of the words and phrases on their list, have them each write a thesis sentence about the attitudes revealed by the language of the programs they watched. ["The excited language used during game shows reflects accurately the drama of the contest," or "The inflated language used on game shows is a pathetic attempt to make unimportant events seem more meaningful."]

When the thesis sentences are completed, have students share them in a class discussion. Ask volunteers to read their thesis sentence and then to read the list of words which supports the thesis.

Now for homework have students write an essay using their thesis sentence as the focus for the essay and the list of relevant language as the main body of detail to support the thesis sentence. They may also use whatever other detail about the program is necessary [plot, setting, costumes] to describe the context in which the language was spoken.

SPECIAL POINTS

This can be a difficult exercise because it calls for some relatively sophisticated analysis of why people repeatedly choose certain words over others. Give this assignment only after the class has had adequate introduction to language choice.

Despite its difficulty, we believe that this exercise is worth the trouble because it makes students conscious of the language with which they are constantly bombarded.

Some students will empathize with the attitudes they perceive in the patterns of language they hear on television while others will criticize these same attitudes. Both points of view are equally appropriate for this assignment.

4 EXPOSITION, ANALYSIS, AND ARGUMENT

This section begins with an essay on how to teach research papers, which includes a number of provocative topics for student research. Then there are two exercises which offer well-defined topics for student analysis. Next, there are five exercises which use journalism as a vehicle for observation, organization, description, interviewing, analysis, and argument. The next three exercises have students examine the relationship between point of view and word choice. Finally, two lengthy exercises introduce students to the analysis of propaganda and logical argument.

To help the students organize their essays, you may wish to distribute the handout on outlines, page 183.

ON TEACHING RESEARCH PAPERS

We would like to share three aspects of teaching research papers which we have found particularly helpful and five possible topics for student research.

MAKE SURE EACH STUDENT DOES EACH STEP

It took us quite a few years of teaching to discover that if we were to successfully teach a class how to do a research paper well, we had to break down the process of writing such a paper into its basic parts (develop a thesis, compile a source list, take notes, develop a thesis sentence, write the outline, write the paper) and then absolutely require that each student do each part and do it properly. Some students try to get out of having to write an outline, or strongly resist the idea of taking notes on index cards. The necessity and reasonableness of such actions, while eminently obvious to us, becomes clear to these students only after they experience the entire process. It took us some years to come up with the courage to be inflexible in these matters, to require that each and every part be handed in with the final paper, and to endure the unpopularity and bitter complaints which often resulted.

MAKE SURE EACH STUDENT UNDERSTANDS
EACH STEP WHILE DOING IT

The second thing we learned was to stay in close touch with each student every step of the way. We found we had to consult with each student about his particular thesis idea, then about his source list, then about his notes, then about his thesis sentence, and then about his outline—in addition to discussing the properties of each with the class as a whole. Often such discussions would be brief, but sometimes they would reveal a fundamental misunderstanding of the process involved which we could then clear up on the spot.

USE THE CLASS MEETINGS
FOR A WRITING WORKSHOP

We found it fairly easy to do this, even with large classes, by assigning the students a relatively long paper and then turning the class periods

131

into a writing workshop. In that way we could make general presentations as required and devote the rest of the class time to individual consultations while the other students did research or wrote in the classroom.

Before we learned the value of this workshop approach, we received from some students spectacularly unsuccessful papers which we later realized were at least partly our fault. Now we deal with problems as they come up, at the same time ensuring that each student understands and properly completes each part. We try to balance the pain of our beginning students' complaints against the pleasure of their final success.

FIVE TOPICS FOR POSSIBLE STUDENT RESEARCH

UNSOLVED MYSTERIES. Have students examine a mystery such as UFO's, the Loch Ness monster, or Atlantis, and report on the nature of the mystery, major efforts to solve it, the results of those efforts, and current opinion about how—or if—the mystery may eventually be resolved.

A CRIME OR SCANDAL OF A CENTURY. What was the Watergate scandal of an earlier time? What mighty personages were shown to have feet of clay? What evil persons committed what sinister crime? What of the Medicis? The Borgias? Ask students to describe the crime, consider the perpetrator, detail events leading up to its discovery and resolution, and report on the crime's ultimate effects or repercussions.

A GREAT DISASTER IN HISTORY. You might suggest the Lusitania, the Hindenburg, Pompeii, the San Francisco Earthquake, the Chicago Fire. Many students enjoy searching for contemporaneous reports and describing the causes and consequences of a disaster.

THE EVOLUTION OF AN INVENTION. Did you know that the first computer filled an entire building but was less sophisticated than a modern-day pocket calculator? Some students enjoy tracing the development of such inventions as airplanes, telephones, or mass-produced books. Others are curious about the development of polio vaccine or the Uncertainty Principle. Ask them to report on the inventor, the events that led up to the invention, and how, once invented, it evolved into its present form.

SOMETHING I'VE ALWAYS WANTED TO KNOW ABOUT. We have yet to find a student who, if skillfully questioned, remains completely incurious about his world. Whether it is gunpowder, Jane Goodall, the Charge of the Light Brigade, making a guitar, or ways to make a million dollars, everybody has at least one thing about which he would like to know more. This is one of our favorite research assignments, even though we have found that going from the general subject to a reasonable thesis idea can be difficult and time-consuming. In our opinion, however, the results justify the extra effort because students themselves experience the process of shaping a broad area which interests them into a well-defined question.

THE TWIN PROBLEM

PURPOSE AND DESCRIPTION

Provides an excellent opportunity for students to practice debate, argument, logic, and outlining on their own and as a group. Students are presented a difficult case in medical ethics (adapted from one taught as part of a course in medical ethics at Harvard Medical School). They are required to decide the proper course of action and to write an essay in support of their decision.

LEVEL   Intermediate and advanced.

CLASS PERIODS   Approximately one week.

ADVANCE PREPARATION

Handout

THE TWIN PROBLEM—CASE DESCRIPTION

You are a highly skilled surgeon with a flourishing practice. You know you are very good at what you do and have earned the respect of your patients.

One day a Mr. and Mrs. Waterhouse come to see you. They are obviously very upset, and tell you they have a problem of life and death and need your help.

The Waterhouses explain that they are the parents of 14 year old twin girls named Irene and Meg. Some years ago Irene contracted a disease of the kidneys, and she has been seriously ill ever since. Her kidneys are now so badly damaged that unless she receives a kidney transplant she will surely die within three months.

Irene is a charming and open girl, full of vitality and intelligence. She is studying piano, and is so good that her teacher feels sure she will have a most successful professional career—if she lives.

The parents tell you—as you already know—that the only kidney transplant which will be successful is one from Irene's identical twin. All other kidney transplants are universally unsuccessful because of rejection by the recipients of the "foreign" tissue. Only Meg's kidney can save Irene's life.

You also know that a kidney transplant between twins is a relatively safe operation. There is some risk, of course, as there is with any major surgery, but it is minimal. Both the donor and the recipient can get along on one kidney apiece.

The obvious solution is for you to transplant one of Meg's kidneys to Irene, and that is what Mr. and Mrs. Waterhouse ask you to do. But, they tell you, there is a serious problem.

Meg has flatly refused to agree to the operation.

Unlike her sister, Meg is depressed, socially backward, and shy. Her parents have focused on Irene's illness and her musical achievements, and Meg feels profoundly rejected.

Meg's parents have told her about the urgent need for the transplant. They have explained that Irene will die unless she is given one of Meg's kidneys. But Meg says she has always hated Irene, who has received much more love and attention than she has, and she—Meg—will certainly do nothing whatsoever to prevent Irene from dying. Every possible device has been used to make Meg change her mind, including extensive psychiatric treatment, but without success.

In desperation, say the Waterhouses, they have come to you for help. In the state in which you practice you are permitted to operate on a person under the age of 18 if his or her parents consent to the operation. The patient, as a minor, has no legal rights in the matter. Mr. and Mrs. Waterhouse say they have decided to ask you to go ahead and perform the operation over Meg's objections in order to save Irene's life. They know you are the best possible surgeon, and say they will do whatever you decide—but they plead with you to decide to operate.

You know:

1. Irene will die if you don't operate.

2. You have the parents' consent to operate.

3. You cannot be prevented either legally or physically from operating.

4. Meg, although only 14, says the operation can take place only if you and her parents resort to physical force to get her

to the hospital because she is absolutely and eternally unwilling to consent of her own free will.

5. Your decision is yours alone to make, and is final.

THE PROBLEM   Will you operate?

RULES   You must accept everything written here as true and unchangeable. You may not invent miracle cures or have a psychiatrist, doctor, or anyone else change Meg's mind at the last minute.

You may be interested to know this is a true story—although a dated one. Today, kidney transplants are possible between people other than identical twins, but at the time this case happened they were not. The names, of course, have been changed.

"The Twin Problem" turns on the issue of conflicting individual rights. Irene wants to live. Meg wants to keep her body from being invaded against her will. The facts of the case are such that your decision will be difficult, but you *must* make a choice. Either you operate on Meg by force or Irene dies.

ACTIVITY

Tell the class as a group that each student has just become a doctor. It is their duty to study the case you are going to present to them and come to a decision about the course of action to be taken. The case is difficult, but each student must make a choice. Read the handout to the class and pass out copies.

The approach we have found most successful is to present the case in class and encourage group discussion. The teacher should remain strictly neutral. If discussion lags, or if the group seems to be unanimous, the teacher should advance the minority viewpoint. Explain that there is no perfect answer, and there is much to be said for both points of view. Students should take notes during the discussion on the main points of both sides of the issue.

Hold extensive classroom discussions of the problem before the students start writing. It is a good idea to allow at least one night for reflection and consultation about the case with family and friends.

After the class discussion, tell the students that each must decide whether or not to operate and write an essay supporting that decision. The essay should include all arguments in favor of the point of view chosen and rebuttals for all arguments contrary to that point of view. The assignment offers an excellent opportunity to assign outlines and to hold classroom debates. Class reactions vary, but we have found The Twin Problem can yield as much as a week's work.

SPECIAL POINTS

While the students go through the experience of choosing sides, the teacher can help them become more aware of the criteria they use to make a decision. Are the decisions based on religious, scientific, or philosophical theories? For example, if a student says, "The human body is sacrosanct," it can be useful to ask *why* it is sacrosanct. Through their responses to such questions students can learn a great deal about themselves and their values.

The powerful attraction of "The Twin Problem" derives from its involvement with a number of emotional issues: sibling rivalry, the importance of human life, and control over one's body. Most cases involving such important issues take a great deal of time to explain, and thus many valuable class periods are used up on simple exposition by the teacher. The Twin Problem, in contrast, can be explained quite quickly. Yet, because the issues involved are so complex and possess so many ramifications, debate can flourish for an extended period of time.

Perhaps as a result of these factors, many students find this exercise particularly interesting. It often moves them out into their community to pose the problem to their friends, their parents, and their doctors. Several students have reported heated debates among doctors, nurses, and patients at their doctor's offices when they have described the case.

It helps keep interest high to explain that this case really did happen. Since the issues involved are so complex and so vital, the case was selected as one of five cases taught at the Harvard Medical School in a course in medical ethics. The fact that this case was studied by people who would actually have to make such decisions lends it importance.

We have found it crucial for the teacher *not* to reveal his own opinion, and *not* to tell the students what happened in the real case, until the assignments are handed in. The teacher's strict neutrality keeps the students from deciding that there is only one "right" answer—and keeps the debates going, too.

137

We feel so strongly about this that we have printed what did happen in the real case on page 187, but urge you to put off looking it up for as long as possible.

We have found that this assignment is most effective if the rules on the assignment sheet are followed closely. We require the student to make a decision because in papers which never take a stand students often allow fuzzy logic to slip through. When a student makes a specific choice, the logical consistencies or inconsistencies are easily examined. We forbid easy ways out of the problem because we feel snap solutions do not contribute much to the learning process.

Emphasize the need for students to treat all the arguments they have heard, pro and con, in their papers. Many students will list all the arguments on one side of the issue but only some on the other side.

To help the students organize their papers, you may wish to distribute the handout on outlines, page 183.

This exercise shows students how a group of people can come up with widely different papers and opinions based on essentially identical information.

Each class comes up with new approaches to "The Twin Problem." That's one of the pleasant aspects of teaching it. To help you the first time you teach it, here are some of the more popular arguments we have encountered:

TO OPERATE:

A human life is at stake—it is a doctor's duty to save lives.

Meg might regret this decision in later life and would accuse her parents and the doctor of making the wrong choice in not requiring her to submit to the operation. After all, she is only 14.

Meg's feelings about Irene are obviously irrationally passionate: why should an irrational person be allowed to—in effect—"kill" another person?

If Meg is not forced to submit, her parents will make her life a thousand times more miserable after Irene dies than it is now, while they will probably be nicer to her if she is operated on.

No one knows how Meg will feel in the end, but with only three months for Irene to live we cannot afford to wait and see: we must operate now.

NOT TO OPERATE:

Everyone—even a 14-year-old—should have the right to his or her own body. Therefore we may not cut Meg open and remove one of her kidneys by force against her will.

If you give someone else control over Meg's body, how can you decide who that person should be?

The first requirement of the Hippocratic oath all doctors take is to do no harm—an operation *could* cause terrible harm to Meg.

Meg could die as a result of the operation. We do not have the right to force her to run that risk.

She will have to be taken to the hospital in a strait jacket or heavily sedated. This could harm her severely psychologically and might affect the physical outcome of the operation as well.

What happens if, later, Meg's only remaining kidney gets infected?

SCHOOL

PURPOSE AND DESCRIPTION

A long-term group exercise in logic and analysis. Students isolate problem areas in their school's organization and function and attempt to formulate viable solutions to these problems.

LEVEL   Intermediate and advanced.

CLASS PERIODS

At least six—can be expanded to an entire quarter's project.

ADVANCE PREPARATION   None.

ACTIVITY

None of us has yet taught at a perfect school. If your school is perfect, skip this exercise. If, however, it is imperfect, read on, for this exercise can benefit your school, your students, and yourself.

Ask your class what things they think are wrong with their school. List every complaint on the chalkboard. Keep listing until the students have run out of complaints. Then ask the class to group related complaints under general topic areas such as physical plant, teaching staff, rules, and so on. Have a student act as recording secretary and rewrite the list on the board by category.

Now ask the class to pick that general category which in their opinion represents the most serious problem area. Have someone copy down all the other areas and then erase them from the board, so only the most serious problem remains.

Now have the group analyze the problem selected. How does it manifest itself? What causes it? When you feel the class has discussed the major points, ask the students if they can come up with any reasonable solutions to the problem. Explain that it is relatively easy to agree that something is a problem, but that it is usually quite hard to analyze a problem and propose viable alternatives for a solution. Nonetheless, this process must take place if things are to get any better.

It has helped us at this point to say to the students that if they can come up with reasonable solutions to any or all of the problems which concern them, we will help them prepare a report for the school administration, and will do what we can to help get their proposals adopted. We have in fact done this, and several useful reforms have been instituted as a result.

Have a student record each proposed solution to the problem on the chalkboard. After a number of suggestions have been recorded, ask the students to analyze the most popular suggestions in realistic terms. If the problem is that the school is too crowded and the proposed solution is to build a new school, is there a reasonable chance that the taxpayers will vote the necessary funds? If the problem is that the school day is too long, is it reasonable to suppose that a school day from 10 a.m. to 11 a.m. will be permitted by the administration? Discard any proposed solutions which appear to the class to be impractical. If viable suggestions remain, get the class to elaborate on them. If not, encourage the students to think of alternatives.

The length of time spent to this point depends entirely on you and your students. It may be one class period, or it may be three or four. When you feel the subject has been adequately covered, ask a group of students to prepare as homework a written report summarizing the class' analysis of the problem and all suggestions relating to the proposed solution which the class feels are feasible.

Numerous ways exist to handle the research and the actual writing of a report by the group assigned the task. Each student can prepare a complete draft; then the group can either meld the drafts together or select the best one from those submitted. Or each student can cover a different aspect of the area assigned to the group, following a sequence the group designs. We have found that groups need surprisingly little guidance in working out the technique best for them.

Meanwhile, continue the in-class discussion. Turn to another general area from the first day's notes, and repeat the process of analyzing and proposing solutions. Then ask a second group to prepare a written report on that general area. Continue this process until all major areas have been covered and each student has helped prepare at least one written report. One or more new major areas may crop up and need to be dealt with in the course of these discussions.

When all reports are completed, duplicate them and discuss the reports one at a time with the class. Have the preparing group rewrite each report as required until the class as a whole is satisfied.

141

When a final written consensus is reached, *if the class agrees*, consolidate all the reports into one package and have each student sign a covering letter to the appropriate administrative authority. You may wish to write a separate accompanying letter yourself—the contents of which, naturally, you would share with the class. Then submit the whole package and see what happens.

SPECIAL POINTS

We have found this to be a fascinating real-life experience. Since the topic is one intimately familiar to the students—their own educational institution—it provides a wealth of material to discuss. The requirement that solutions be feasible is in itself realistic, and promotes practical, constructive analysis. The written report is a natural outgrowth of the exercise, and serves to focus discussion and encourage precision.

As is unfortunately so often true in life, many of the problems that come up may not lend themselves to easy, reasonable solutions. Some may appear to the group (and to you) as insoluble. The process of analysis which leads to that conclusion is a useful one, and a greater knowledge of the challenges facing their school and their society often helps students be more tolerant and understanding.

We are fully aware that people in authority at some schools would react extremely badly to a written report from a class on problems facing the school, even if that report were highly constructive. Naturally only you can decide whether or not you wish to undertake this potentially hazardous project. It is possible to do essentially the same exercise without giving the final report to anyone. However, such an approach makes the project lose much of its impact and appeal to the students. Also, copies of the report may turn up in the administration's hands anyway.

In any reasonable school, we believe the fact that a class worked as a group to attempt to create practical solutions to legitimate problems will be recognized for the positive and constructive effort that it is.

One of the things we most enjoy about this assignment is how closely its development parallels the development of similar analyses required throughout life. Leaders and followers emerge, factions rise up, arguments erupt, and acceptable compromises appear at the last possible moment. In some ways it is not "fair" in the typical classroom meaning of that term. Some students will manage to avoid doing a great deal of work, while others will elect an involvement far beyond anything you have asked. The group process requires that everyone agree on generalities, specifics, and even individual words and phrases. Students write, rewrite, and spend time with dictionaries and thesauruses. Perhaps most important, students usually come to believe that the words they choose may have a significant impact on the shape of their own existence. Writing class changes from what sometimes seems an abstract, separate experience to one that is an organic part of their lives.

We do everything we can to have the actual report writing take place as homework, outside of the classroom. The student groups find time to meet before school starts, during free periods, at lunch, or after school. Sometimes they are unable to work out a sufficient block of mutually convenient time suitable for their needs. If this happens, we wait until everyone in the class has been assigned to a group and then allow the entire class to spend one or more class periods working on the group reports. In such cases we preserve order but do not enter into the group process itself.

If you wish, this exercise can take up an entire quarter or even semester. You can move from small reports to consolidated reports to final reports. Students can interview interested parties—other students, teachers, parents, administrators, alumni. They can develop research projects in the field of education, study various teaching philosophies, visit other schools, and so on. Such an approach is particularly appropriate for an advanced class.

The teacher should be extremely careful not to project his own views on the class. It is awfully tempting to voice one's own pet solutions and convince the students that those are the answer. But the teacher who succumbs to this temptation destroys the learning process for the students. He also destroys any chance of the class' developing what may well be superior solutions to the problems.

The teacher can best serve his students by moderating the discussion, keeping things on the track, making sure each student has a chance to be heard, recognizing and encouraging consensus, and fostering the analytic process.

143

FROM THE NEWSPAPER

INTRODUCTION

The five exercises which follow are designed as part of a course in expository writing rather than as part of a course in journalism. The various journalistic forms have been adapted to serve as vehicles to promote observation and description and to provide opportunities for work in organization of material, outlining, and analysis.

Nonetheless, enough of the basic journalism forms remain to provide an introduction to that medium. Statistics reveal the dreary fact that the average American adult reads less than two books a year. Many students will confine their adult reading to the daily newspaper. If they do, these exercises will give them a greater understanding of what they choose to read.

THE DISPUTE

PURPOSE AND DESCRIPTION

An exercise to promote careful observation and precise description. The teacher has an argument with another person in front of the class. After the other person leaves, the teacher asks each student to write a detailed description of the dispute and the other person involved. This is Part I of the five-part "From the Newspaper" series. Please see the preceding Introduction to the series.

LEVEL   Can be adapted to any level. See SPECIAL POINTS.

CLASS PERIODS   One.

ADVANCE PREPARATION

Arrange for a friend who is a stranger to the class to argue with you during the class. Agree on a specific time for the argument to take place and on the precise nature of the argument: a lost car key? a flunked offspring? a minor rudeness? an unpaid debt? Gauge the severity and drama of the argument to the excitability of the class and to your friend's acting ability.

ACTIVITY

Arrange for your friend to argue with you in the middle of a routine class. As soon as your friend leaves, tell the students that what they have just seen was prearranged and was designed to test their powers of observation.

Tell the students not to discuss the incident with one another. Ask them instead to write individual eyewitness reports in class on exactly what happened and on the appearance of the other disputant.

After the students have finished, have your friend return to the classroom and repeat the argument as precisely as possible. Then let your students observe your friend's appearance at leisure. Have them compare their written descriptions to the reality of your friend and the reenactment.

In follow-up discussion, ask the students if they can remember being at a newsworthy event [an accident, a demonstration, a ceremony, a concert] and then reading about it later in a newspaper. Encourage them to talk about the differences between what they experienced and what they later read. Then ask them if they found some of the same kinds of differences in their own descriptions of the argument when compared with the reenacted incident. Help them see that a reporter must become aware of his or her own prejudices and consciously try to overcome them in writing a story.

SPECIAL POINTS

This exercise illuminates how what we see is affected by who we are and what we care about. When the papers are compared, the first thing students notice is the differences in what they perceived. One will describe your friend's face, another will focus on what happened, and somebody else will write about the anger that you displayed. This is a good opportunity to encourage students to examine how what they personally felt during the dispute colored their subsequent reports. What did they choose to emphasize? Why?

For beginning students, consider having your friend dress in unusual and highly noticeable clothing. For more advanced students, develop a more complex series of actions up to and including extensive dialogue. Be very sure that you can precisely duplicate the episode so your students have an accurate reproduction against which to compare their written descriptions. Replicating the dispute precisely is harder than it may at first appear, so practice in advance and be alert to any changes in the real event which differ from the program.

You may preface this exercise with "Quick Study," page 26.

NEWS STORY

PURPOSE AND DESCRIPTION

To practice the descriptive technique necessary to write a straightforward news story, each student is asked to write in the form of a newspaper article a real incident which actually happened to him. This is Part II of the five-part "From the Newspaper" series. (Please see the Introduction to this series on page 144.)

LEVEL   Beginning and intermediate.

CLASS PERIODS   One.

ADVANCE PREPARATION   Bring a newspaper to class.

ACTIVITY

Select a well written news report on a topic of current student interest and read it to the class. Then, using the report as an example, discuss the nature of a news story with the students.

You may wish to point out that a news story is about something which is currently happening. A news story should answer the classic six journalism questions: who, what, when, where, why, and how. One of the key attributes of a newspaper story is that a reference must be given in the article for any fact which the reporter has not personally witnessed. A news story has little description and few adjectives. With extremely rare exceptions, it is not written in the first person.

When you feel the class has grasped the essential characteristics of a news story, read the opening four paragraphs of your sample article to the class a second time. Have a student write the new information in each sentence on the chalkboard. If the story is properly written, the opening sentence will give a general idea of the content of the story, and each subsequent sentence will add new and progressively less important details.

After discussing this technique with the class—and perhaps examining one or two other news articles to clarify the technique—ask the students, as homework, to pick an incident which actually happened to them and to write it in the form of a news story. Remind students to use the same writing techniques discussed in class. Tell the students that they should make the incidents which are subjects of their stories sound current even if the event happened a long time ago. Advise students to start with a headline, and then proceed by answering the six questions.

SPECIAL POINTS

This assignment differs from "The Dispute"—Part I of this series—because it concentrates on *method* of presentation. There is no way for the teacher to evaluate the accuracy of the student's observations because the teacher is usually not familiar with the event the student chooses to describe. We have found this lack of knowledge on the teacher's part an asset because it forces us to focus exclusively on journalistic technique. Consequently we are able to evaluate the student's mastery of the technique and pinpoint areas of difficulty without being distracted by concern for accuracy.

If students say, "Nothing ever happens to me," remind them that they may draw upon any incident which happened to them any time from birth onwards, as long as the incident is written up as if it were currently happening.

To illustrate the kind of distance a reporter should maintain from his story, you may want to ask the students to make up a few headlines in class before starting the assignment. A headline such as, "Johnny Ties Own Sneakers for First Time; Mother Delighted" will help them grasp the concept of journalistic distance.

We tell students to start with a headline in doing the homework assignment so they will have a clear understanding of the purpose of their story. Without a headline, a student's story can be diffuse and unfocused.

One area of possible difficulty is the concept of sources. Beginning students tend to write news articles in the fashion of short fiction stories. You may wish to point out the importance of quotes in this regard. Explain that "Mr. Henderson was heartbroken" is suitable for a short story, but a news article must read, " ' I am heartbroken,' Mr. Henderson said."

Another area that may need extra emphasis is the timeliness of a news story. Often it can be useful to point out phrases such as: ". . . the investigation is continuing . . .", "tomorrow the board will . . .",

148

". . . nothing more is known at this time . . .", "an announcement is expected shortly . . ." These help the students see that news stories are written about things *as they happen*. A news story rarely comes complete with a beginning, middle, and end all tied neatly together.

One thing to be alert for is a student who confuses print journalism with radio or TV journalism. Such a student will write, "Now let's go to our man on the spot," or "We'll have details on the hour."

After the students have completed this exercise, if you think they need more practice in writing news stories, you may want to ask them to rewrite their description of "The Dispute" (the previous exercise) in the form of a newspaper article.

THE INTERVIEW

PURPOSE AND DESCRIPTION

An exercise in precise description which requires students to compare a real person with a preconceived type. This is Part III of the five-part "From the Newspaper" series. (Please see the Introduction to this series on page 144.)

LEVEL   Intermediate and advanced.

CLASS PERIODS   Two or more.

ADVANCE PREPARATION

Handout

INTERVIEWS

Before holding an interview, write out a list of questions you want to ask so that you don't forget an important one. Bring your list of questions to the interview, and put a check mark next to each when your subject has answered it. This way you'll be sure you've covered everything.

Schedule the interview so that you and your subject will have enough time together. It's better to schedule too much time (you can always stop early) than too little. Try to arrange things so you won't be interrupted. If people are walking in and out, it's hard to keep the interview going smoothly.

During the interview you should record your subject's answers to your questions. Accuracy and direct quotes lend vividness to your writing. You may want to take notes or use a tape recorder. If you take notes, you have to write fast. If you use a tape recorder, you probably will have to take notes from the tape later.

Try to keep your questions objective and non-directive. This will help you uncover not only the information you specifically request but also other information you may not have expected but which may prove especially useful. Here are some examples of directive and non-directive questions:

DIRECTIVE	NON-DIRECTIVE
Do you break the speed limit a lot?	What do you think of the 55mph speed limit?
I suppose you're a political conservative.	What are your political views: liberal, conservative, or somewhere in between?
Are you one of those male chauvinist pigs?	What do you think is the proper role of women in our society?

When you ask a question, pursue the answer you get. Don't be content with general answers. Often the most specific and revealing information is obtained if you follow a small general lead offered by your subject. For example:

Q. What do you do in your spare time?

A. I putter around the house.

Q. Doing what?

A. I clean up a lot.

Q. Why?

A. I have eight kids and there's always something to clean.

Q. Eight kids! Why did you decide to have eight kids?

A. I was an only child and very lonely. Since I was so miserable as a child, my husband and I wanted our children to have lots of companions.

A good interview can have the quality of a good conversation. If you and your subject feel genuine interest in one another's experiences, you may well end up relating to one another in a personal way.

ACTIVITY

Ask the class to think of a number of categories of people and write each on the chalkboard. Possible categories include job descriptions [corporation executive, truck driver, librarian], political and philosophical designations [feminist, right winger], and physical types [80-year-old, beautiful woman, athlete].

Then ask each student to pick a category which represents a group of people with which he is *not* familiar and yet about which he would like to know more. Ask each student to spend 15 minutes listing characteristics he would expect to find in a person belonging to this category. The list should include guesses as to: his/her current family status, occupation, hobbies, political and social opinions, education, family background, and outlook on life. For example, one might characterize a librarian as: spinster, collects antique bottles, birdwatcher, Democrat, favors government spending programs to help the poor, feels young people are less respectful than in her day, has a master's degree in library science, is quietly pessimistic, enjoys rare books, is fussy about details, and prides herself on her knowledge of little-known facts.

After the writing time is over, tell the students that as homework they are to interview a real person who falls into the category each has chosen. They must find an appropriate subject with whom they are *not* personally acquainted prior to the interview. They may use their families, friends, and fellow students to locate such a person. Explain that the purpose of the interview is to determine in what ways the real person fits their preconceptions and in what ways the real person differs from their preconceptions. Then they are to write an essay comparing and contrasting their imaginary person with the real person they interviewed.

Explain that the *content* of the interview should cover the following areas: current family status, occupation, hobbies, political and social opinions, education, and family background. What is the subject's outlook on life? What makes him happy? What does he want? What does he fear? Students should observe and record in a notebook the subject's physical appearance, clothing, characteristic gestures, and attitude throughout the interview.

If your students are unfamiliar with interviewing techniques, you can help them practice through role-playing in the classroom. Be the interviewee and ask the class to interview you. This provides a good opportunity to help students appreciate the validity of non-directive questioning.

You may wish to spend two class periods introducing this assignment and role-playing practice interviews if your students are unfamiliar with interviewing techniques.

After the students have completed their interviews and their essays, spend at least one class session reading the results aloud. Ask the class to discuss the relationship between the quality of the interview and the quality of the final essay. Is there a connection? Encourage each author to share with the class what went on in the interview. Ask the students to exchange information about which questions were particularly fruitful and which were not. See if the class can develop useful generalizations about both kinds of questions.

It is also interesting to discuss the class' feelings about the relationship of their imaginary people to their real-life subjects. In what ways were the students surprised? In what ways did they find their expectations corresponded to the reality? What conclusions did they draw from the experience?

SPECIAL POINTS

This is a complex assignment, but it is one of the best ways we know to make students aware of their own preconceptions and to help them keep these preconceptions from coming between themselves and their subjects. The need to compare assumptions with reality forces students to recognize the difference between an abstraction and a real person.

It is important to have students choose a category with which they are *not* familiar and to interview someone they do not know. If the only thing the student knows about the interviewee is that he is a member of an unfamiliar category, the similarities and differences between the real and imagined person will be contrasted sharply in the course of the interview.

This assignment shows students that general ideas are not as effective as specifics. It points up the need for texture and detail. The most successful interviews and subsequent essays will be those in which the author makes full use of specific detail to illustrate imagined or observed general characteristics of the person interviewed.

If you have particularly uncertain students, you may wish to preface this assignment with a typical school interviewing assignment [a new student, a parent, or a member of the maintenance crew].

153

We feel it is a good idea not to reveal the entire object of the exercise until after the students have completed the 15-minute written descriptions of the category each has chosen. We believe it is important that students generate as unadulterated preconceptions as possible.

Two or more students should not be allowed to conduct a joint interview if they happen to have chosen the same category. Students should work out their own interviews in their individual ways, undistracted and unaided by the presence of a friend.

It is often a good idea to help the students rehearse the manner in which they request the actual interview. Suggest that they say something like, "As a school/college project I have been asked to interview someone who is a carpenter/ an older person/ a Democrat."

Since the homework assignment involves several steps (locate an appropriate subject, conduct an interview, write an essay comparing and contrasting the subject to the author's preconceptions), allow several days for its completion.

To help the students organize their essays, you may wish to distribute the handout on outlines, page 183.

There are two items on the handout sheet which need special emphasis. Make a point of encouraging students to write out a list prior to the interview of all the important questions they would like to ask, and advise them to refer perfectly openly to that list during the interview to make certain that they have covered all the questions on it.

We also suggest that you check each student's plans to record the content of the interview itself. Most beginning students intend to rely solely on memory, an obvious error.

You may wish to read one or two interviews to the class from *Working* by Studs Terkel as examples of superlative interviewing and reporting.

When you ask the students to list various kinds of people at the start of this exercise, one or more relatively inaccessible categories may come up [an astronaut, the oldest man in the world, a murderer]. Be sure to delete any hard-to-locate types from the list on the board before you ask the students to pick one to write about.

REVIEWS

PURPOSE AND DESCRIPTION

An exercise in descriptive writing and argument. Students write a review of a movie, play, television program, or other performance. This is Part IV of the five-part "From the Newspaper" series. (Please see the Introduction to this series on page 144.)

LEVEL   Any.

CLASS PERIODS   One.

ADVANCE PREPARATION

Bring a few sample reviews to class.

ACTIVITY

Explain the concept of a review to the class. You may wish to point out that most reviews of a performance describe the event in enough detail so that a person who did not see it would have a good idea of what took place and would have an opinion as to how successfully or interestingly it was done.

Read your sample reviews to the class and discuss the reviewer's point of view about the performance and the performers. How does the reviewer get this point of view across to the reader?

Then tell students they are to act as reviewers for the school newspaper (whether or not there is one). Ask them to review a performance about which they have strong feelings *before* they attend. Whether it is a movie, play, television program, record album, or concert, they should care about it and want to convince others to share their point of view.

Explain that the actual process they will need to go through to write an effective review is as follows:

1. Observe a performance.

2. Evaluate its content and form in terms of its purpose and by comparing and contrasting it to other like performances in the same field.

3. Take a point of view about the performance.

4. Analyze the performance in terms of your point of view.

5. Write up your analysis so as to convince your reader to share your point of view about the performance.

Tell the students to be careful in their reviews to bolster the point of view with specific, concrete detail from the performance being reviewed. Instead of simply saying, "The movie was just as scary as the ads said it would be," they should tell the reader why. Were there monsters from the deep? Sudden murders? Ghosts? How did the director use light? What about the pace of the action? What about the sound track?

SPECIAL POINTS

Successful professional reviewers almost invariably have strong points of view about their topics. We ask our students to review performances about which they feel strongly in advance—whether because of the star, the subject matter, the writer, or the director—so that they will have a point of view from which to write their reviews. It does not matter whether their strong feelings are positive or negative, nor does it matter whether or not the performance makes them change their minds.

We have not emphasized some of the technical aspects of a review in this exercise [the need to give exact title, author, names of major performers, directors, producers] because this is primarily a writing exercise in argument. However, we do mention these elements in our discussion of the sample reviews we bring to class.

Depending on the sophistication of the students, we also discuss the importance of the reviewer's audience and the ways in which a review in a magazine like *Family Circle* differs significantly from one on the same subject in *Hollywood Variety* or *The New Yorker*. We specifically tell the students that they are reviewing for the real or imaginary school paper so they will have a clear idea of their audience.

You may want to tell the students to consider Goethe's three questions: "What is the artist trying to do? How well has he done it? Was it worth doing?"

If your class is fairly advanced, you may want to encourage the writers to examine the fundamental themes of the pieces in question and how effectively the themes were realized.

Many students do not understand the evaluation function of a review. They think all they should do is say the performance was good or

156

the performance was bad. Help them see that good reviews go beyond simple praise or criticism to explain why a performance was successful or unsuccessful. Further, most reviews are not all praise or all blame. They find well-done features in a boring performance and boring features in a well-done performance.

One problem in having students write reviews is that many may not appreciate the importance of specialized knowledge on the reviewer's part. Try to encourage students to review in an area with which they are familiar. A student who never listens to classical music should not attempt to review a new performance of Mahler's *Fifth Symphony* even if it should happen to be being conducted by a favorite rock star.

You will have an easier time evaluating the review if you have seen the performance in question, but it is not essential for you to do so.

EDITORIALS

PURPOSE AND DESCRIPTION

To develop argumentative skills, students are asked to write an editorial on a topic of interest to them. Then each is asked to write a letter to the editor rebutting one of the other students' editorials. This is Part V of the five-part "From the Newspaper" series. (Please see the Introduction to this series on page 144.)

LEVEL   Any.

CLASS PERIODS   Two or three.

ADVANCE PREPARATION

Bring to class some examples of editorials from the school paper or other local papers.

ACTIVITY

Drawing upon the sample editorials you have brought for examples, discuss the nature of an editorial with the class. Point out that the classic editorial is a short, persuasive essay concerning a situation, issue, or event about which the editor holds a strong opinion. It usually begins by describing the subject in general terms. Then it elaborates on what the editor considers the subject's main points through the use of specific, factual detail. It ends by stating the opinion of the editor as to the subject's justice, significance, or purpose.

After discussing the nature of an editorial, pick a topic of current student interest. It may be a school rule, some other local issue, or a development in national or international affairs. If news is slack, you could try gun control, whether or not students should be required to attend school until the age of 16, the use of animals for scientific research, corporal punishment in schools, or the death penalty.

Instruct each student to take a point of view about the subject chosen and write as persuasive an editorial as possible in support of this point of view. Tell your students that the main purpose of an editorial is to persuade others to agree with the author's point of view. This is most often done through the careful selection of good supporting detail. If, as they write, the students keep in mind a reader who disagrees with their point of view, their editorials will probably be more effective. Editorials which appeal only to supporters of the author's position miss out on an opportunity to convert opponents. Editorials which seek to convert will still serve to reinforce the opinion of supporters. The editorials may be done in class or assigned as homework.

When the students have finished their editorials, you may want to have them read their papers to the class. Ask the other students to evaluate each editorial's persuasiveness, irrespective of whether or not they agree with the author's point of view.

To help students gain a clearer understanding of the editorial form, pass out the student editorials at random and tell each student to write a letter to an imaginary editor disagreeing with that editorial. Students should rebut the editorial systematically, point by point.

To help students focus on point of view, ask them to pretend, as they write their letters, that they are a particular kind of person who would be expected to disagree with the editorial. For example, an editorial in favor of space exploration could be rebutted by a person who was head of an organization trying to get more government assistance for poor people. Or, an editorial favoring higher wages for farm workers could be opposed by a person who owned a farm. You can assign appropriate people or the students can think of their own. This can be done in class or as homework.

SPECIAL POINTS

As a follow-up assignment to this exercise, you can ask students to rebut a real editorial, with which they disagree, by writing a letter to the editor. If well written, such a letter might even get published.

If you choose to discuss the chosen editorial topic extensively in class before your students write about it, this assignment can also be an exercise in organization, for most of the main arguments will have been covered. If you do not discuss the subject extensively beforehand, then the emphasis of the exercise may shift to the author's resourcefulness and imagination in coming up with important points to bolster the main thesis. Base the extent of the class discussion on the abilities and interests of your students. Some students need to have extensive preliminary discussion or they "don't have anything to say," while other students prefer to think up all the arguments themselves.

By asking students to rebut another's editorial, you give them further practice in analyzing persuasive writing. A well-written editorial will be harder to rebut than a poorly-written one because a good editorial is logical, anticipates alternative arguments, and refutes them in advance. The actual letter-writing process provides further practice in argument.

We are careful to require that each student have a very specific point of view when he rebuts his classmate's work. This enables students to gain further understanding of how a strong point of view shapes an argument.

Remind the students to use the library when necessary to seek facts to support their points of view in both the editorial and the rebuttal letters.

To help the students organize their editorials, you may wish to distribute the handout on outlines, page 183.

INDUCED CONCLUSIONS

PURPOSE AND DESCRIPTION

An exercise in the use of selected details to induce a predetermined conclusion in the reader's mind. Can also be used to teach effective description. Students write brief descriptions to create a specific effect.

LEVEL   Beginning and intermediate.

CLASS PERIODS   One.

ADVANCE PREPARATION

Handout

INDUCED CONCLUSIONS

A. Elaine does not like the boy she is with.

B. Elaine looked over his shoulder and waved frantically to another boy in a red convertible. "Huh?" she said vaguely. . . "What was that you were saying?"

A and B are two different ways of writing about essentially the same thing. A tells the reader something but doesn't show him anything. B shows it all and the reader draws his own conclusion. The author has shaped the events in B in such a way that the reader will draw the conclusion the author intends—the conclusion stated in A.

Listed below are several conclusions. For each conclusion write a few sentences of the type found in B above—sentences which make the reader come to the same conclusion by himself. You do not have to do the conclusions in the order listed below. Be sure, however, to write the appropriate conclusion above each group of descriptive sentences.

1. The puppy is very hungry.

2. Bill hates school.

3. The librarian likes the movies.

4. The concert bored the musician.

161

5. The store manager wears beautiful clothes.

6. The old man knows a lot about farming.

7. My uncle Tom is stealing from his office.

8. Jack is a real creep.

9. She is mad at her mother.

10. I like Marie but am afraid to show it.

11. Nobody likes Anna.

12. The referee was unfair.

ACTIVITY

Distribute and explain the assignment. It may be done in class or as homework.

SPECIAL POINTS

This may be the first time some students really understand how a writer can affect a reader's opinion without overtly stating what he wants that opinion to be. Many beginning and intermediate writers simply tell the reader what to think, a technique which can be both offensive and ineffective. This exercise helps students understand that it is often better to *show* a reader that something is so rather than to *tell* a reader that something is so.

Once the students have mastered the difference between telling and showing, you may want to discuss how the Type B sentences create a vivid and specific picture, allowing the reader to actively experience the point the writer is trying to make. Most students will agree that descriptions which give the reader the texture and flavor of an experience not only get the idea across more effectively but are also more enjoyable to read.

162

DISTORTION

PURPOSE AND DESCRIPTION

An exercise showing that writers select words for their connotative meanings in order to affect readers. Together, students read a gossip tabloid, a movie fan magazine, or a similar publication and analyze the particular language used to slant and distort a story for sensational purposes. Then, using the same language, students write a description of a small incident which is staged in the classroom.

LEVEL   Beginning and intermediate.

CLASS PERIODS   Two.

ADVANCE PREPARATION   Obtain a copy of a magazine written in sensational style. Select three or four short articles and several headlines from other longer articles which use language for sensational purposes. Duplicate these articles and headlines for the class.

Before class ask two students to help improvise a small incident which can be used by the class as the basis for a descriptive news story in the style of the magazine you are about to analyze. Some suggested incidents are a casual greeting or parting, making a date or an appointment, or borrowing a quarter. The scene should not last more than a minute and should be purposely neutral, underplayed, and unexaggerated in tone. The purpose of this neutrality is to have the writers, not the actors, exaggerate and distort the ordinary incident.

ACTIVITY   Day One

Distribute the handouts of articles and headlines from the magazine you have chosen. Explain that the students are to read them silently and underline those words, phrases, and sentences which they feel distort, exaggerate, or in some way slant the facts for sensational purposes. To give students an idea of what to look for, you may first want to do this aloud with the class using one of the articles.

When the class has finished underlining the articles and headlines, compile on the chalkboard a list from the articles of words and phrases typical of the magazine's style. Discuss with the class how these words

163

and phrases are used to manipulate the reader through the power and impact of their connotations. Ask the class to identify some of the connotations of those words which have strong emotional effects [secret, miracle, romance, dream, heartless, shocking]. What are the underlying associations connected with these words and phrases?

Next tell the class that they are to use the same manipulative language to write a short news story for the same magazine they have been analyzing. The story should be based on the incident which they are about to witness. Ask the two student volunteers to stage their "incident." Tell the class to make notes after they have watched the staged incident. The notes will help students remember the facts when they write the story for homework. Remind them that the language of the news story is to have sensational connotations for the reader.

Day Two

Have students share their completed news stories. Discuss the variety of points of view about the same incident which can be achieved through manipulating language.

SPECIAL POINTS

Students enjoy gaining an understanding of how language manipulates. This understanding enables them to be more discerning when faced with the highly connotative language of media and advertising, and makes them feel more powerful in that they can use this language themselves.

This is a beginning exercise to help students understand how style is determined by the intended audience of a piece of writing. "Audiences," page 119, is a good assignment to follow this exercise because it further develops the idea that style and audience are connected.

THE LANGUAGE OF ADVERTISING

PURPOSE AND DESCRIPTION

To show students how a writer's purpose and intended audience shape his approach and word choice. Students examine a number of similar advertisements from a variety of popular magazines and then create an ad of their own.

LEVEL   Beginning and intermediate.

CLASS PERIODS   One-quarter plus one.

ADVANCE PREPARATION

Collect and bring to class for your own reference examples of advertisements for similar products from several different magazines [automobile ads from *Time, Seventeen,* and *Road and Track*]. If your class is large, also bring an opaque projector. Use this to display examples of ads to the class.

ACTIVITY   Day One

At the end of a class period ask each student to bring in two advertisements for the same kind of product from two different types of magazines [a Cadillac ad from *Time* and a Mustang ad from *Seventeen*]. Allow a few days for them to do this.

Day Two

Select from your students' examples several ads for the same kind of product. Identify the magazines from which each ad was taken. Then choose one ad and discuss with the class what they know about the audience of the magazine in which it appeared. [At which social or economic groups does the magazine aim? Does it appeal to particular interest groups? What are some values its readers apparently share?]

With that audience in mind, discuss how the creator of the ad tried to appeal to that audience. Did he use abstract or concrete language [a car with "style" and "class," or a car with "bucket seats" and "power steering"]? What was the connotative impact of the language? [What is

165

the difference between shopping for "class" or buying "power steering"?] How did the picture's subject, color, focus, and background reinforce the implications of the text? Make sure the class recognizes not only to what audience but to what particular feelings or desires of that audience the ad was directed. Throughout the discussion make explicit the ways that the ad's sales approach, through language and pictorial detail, attempts to connect with these feelings or desires.

Then for homework ask students to design an ad for a product in which they really believe. It may be a fictional product or an actual favorite.

Remind your students that a good ad makes only one point. Because all of us are exposed to a number of advertisements every day, we are normally unable to remember more than one basic idea from even the most effective ad.

Have students begin by naming the type of magazine and audience to which their ad will be directed. Next have them design the picture for the ad. This may be an actual picture or a detailed written description of a picture (if the latter, the description should state whether the picture is a drawing or photograph, whether it is in black and white or color, and should give the details of the foreground and background). Have students then write an appropriate headline and, finally, the accompanying text. Remind them that these ads are to be for magazines only, not for radio or television.

SPECIAL POINTS

This is a good introduction to concepts of word choice and connotative language because advertising text is usually simple and closely connected to its visual illustration. For more visually oriented students, make sure that the picture plays a central role in the ads you choose to discuss. The illustration will help them see graphically the relationships among the writer's purpose, his perception of the audience's feelings and desires, and his word choice.

We bring our own sample ads to class for reference and as a resource to demonstrate clearly contrasting approaches. However, we prefer to use our students' samples for class discussion whenever possible to make the students feel more fully included in the process of examination and discovery.

166

INTRODUCTION TO PROPAGANDA

PURPOSE AND DESCRIPTION

To introduce students to various techniques of propaganda. A discussion of some basic propaganda techniques is followed by a class exercise in writing propaganda.

LEVEL   Intermediate and advanced.

CLASS PERIODS   Two.

ADVANCE PREPARATION

First handout

TECHNIQUES OF PROPAGANDA

If you want to make your reader react favorably to your subject, try:

Glittering generalities	"the most wonderful"
	"our nation's finest"
	"once-in-a-lifetime opportunity"
Slanting material	Emphasize material which supports your point and leave out material which harms it.
Appeal to authority	"doctors prefer . . ."
	"a leading expert says . . ."
	"Abraham Lincoln always maintained . . ."
Appeal to tradition	"tried and true"
	"our firm, which has been in business for over 100 years . . ."
	"like grandmother used to make . . ."

167

Appeal to large numbers	"50,000 people can't be wrong"
	"everyone in town is doing it"
	"4 out of 5 surveyed agree"
Appeal to popular passions	"In the spirit of the American Revolution . . ."
	"If you believe in giving everyone an equal chance, then you'll agree . . ."
	"Financial security can be yours with the help of . . ."
Ceremony and setting (an exclusively visual technique)	A new car photographed against the background of a stately mansion.
	A religious symbol used as part of an advertising display.
	A television newscaster reporting in front of an enlarged photograph of the U.S. Capitol.

If you want to make your reader react *unfavorably* to your subject, try:

Name calling	"traitor!"
	"babbling fool"
	"bra-burning women's libber"
Personal attack	"What can you expect from a proven liar?"
	"He's always been a troublemaker."
	"She never thinks of anyone but herself."
Damning origins	"You New Yorkers are all alike."
	"Surely you don't think the big oil interests want to *preserve* the environment?"

	"She never even made it through high school—what does she know about it?"
Creating misgivings	"Just imagine what awful things might happen if . . ."
	"I hear he may be secretly working for the other side."
	"They say lots of people dislike her—there must be some reason."
Colored words	If a person is stubborn, is he "firm" or "pig-headed"?
	Is a car an "elegant sedan" or a "gas-eating monster"?
	If someone says something which is untrue, is it an "accidental mis-statement" or is it a "deliberate lie"?
Charged words	"All mothers know . . ."
	"Every red-blooded American agrees . . ."
	"Only Communists think . . ."

Second Handout

AN INTRODUCTION TO
THE KNIGHTS OF THE KU KLUX KLAN

After the cannon fell silent and peace descended upon the battlefields of the great Civil War, there came a dark and infamous chapter of American History called "The Reconstruction." From this era, this abyss of utter human misery and despair, there arose like the morning sun the KU KLUX KLAN. This Order provided for the people of the South the leadership and rallying point to begin their long and arduous struggle to regain their lost dignity. The noble and glorious ride of the Ku Klux Klan of the Reconstruction era is immortalized by its achievements. No errors

169

of omission or commission by prejudiced historians can dim the lustre of its deeds, or rob it of its rightful place in history as the saviour of the nation; for had there been no ride of the Ku Klux Klan there would not today be fifty stars in the flag that graces the dome of our Nation's Capitol.

To keep alive the memory of the original Klan and the principles, traditions and institutions which they risked their lives to preserve for themselves and for posterity, the men of today, who appreciate their patriotic and chivalric work, have established a living, lasting memorial to them by the organization of the United Klans of America, Knights of the Ku Klux Klan. The United Klans of America, KKK, is a national fraternal order composed of real American manhood of the nation who uncompromisingly believe in perpetual preservation of the fundamental principles, ideals and institutions of the pure Anglo-Saxon civilization and all the fruits thereof.[1]

ACTIVITY   Day One

Begin the exploration of propaganda by passing out the first handout sheet and discussing the techniques of propaganda. In the course of the discussion, encourage the students to give numerous examples of each technique from their own experience or imagination. Then pass out the second handout sheet and ask the students to identify each of the techniques used in the Klan introduction. This will probably consume an entire class period.

Day Two

Review the same techniques of propaganda covered during the first day of discussion. Then tell the class you are going to give them a set of facts on which to practice those techniques. Tell them to imagine a clear glass bottle containing 20 plain white pills and labeled "Smith's Headache Remedy." Have the students imagine that they are the advertising agency on the Smith account. Give them 15 minutes to write sentences

---

1. From a pamphlet of the same name prepared by the Knights of the Ku Klux Klan.

supporting the use of the pills. They are to use as many of the propaganda techniques you have been examining with them as possible. Ask the students to be as persuasive as they can. Tell them that the most effective approach will be to develop a specific point of view. A series of unrelated positive (or negative) points will not be as impressive as a series of points which supports one major theme. [All the positive points could be related to the relief of pain, or to the speed of the remedy, or to the strength of the remedy, or to its low cost.]

At the end of 15 minutes, tell the students they have now become members of a team trying to prevent drug abuse. Say they now have 15 minutes to write material denouncing the pills, again using as many different propaganda techniques as they can, and again being as persuasive as possible. When they have finished, have students read their papers to the class. In class discussion compare and contrast the techniques used in the papers to determine their effectiveness.

SPECIAL POINTS

If you have several different magazines on hand in the classroom, you will be able to use the advertisements as resource material for examples of each kind of propaganda. We prefer to get the examples from the students directly, and use the magazines only if the classroom examples dry up.

The terms used on the propaganda list are from *Fallacy: The Counterfeit of Argument,* by W. Ward Fearnside and William B. Holther (New Jersey: Prentice-Hall, Inc., 1959).

A CAUSE

PURPOSE AND DESCRIPTION

A lengthy exercise in logic, analysis, and propaganda. Students analyze the literature of two groups with opposing views on a specific political, economic, or social issue; interview a spokesperson for one of the groups; and make an oral presentation to the class on the logic of that point of view and on the propaganda techniques used by the group to advance that point of view. Then they read two more pieces of literature on the same issue, take a position of their own on the issue, and write an essay in support of that position which they attempt to make as logical and free of propaganda as possible.

LEVEL   Intermediate and advanced.

CLASS PERIODS

Three weeks (allow one or two additional weeks of work outside of class).

ADVANCE PREPARATION

The preceding exercise, "Introduction to Propaganda," page 167.

Before Day One, make copies of the two handouts below: "Tests of Logic" and "Advertising Needs No Apologists."

Before Day Two, make copies of the handout on page 178: "A Cause—Oral Report."

Before Day Four, make copies of the two handouts on pages 182–183: "A Cause—Essay" and "Outlines."

Handouts for Day One

TESTS OF LOGIC

When you analyze an argument, test it to see if it is logical. Include these tests in your analysis.

A.   *EVIDENCE*

1. Is it *accurate*?

If your mother says she won't raise your allowance because you spent all your money on junk food last week, but you didn't, then her evidence is not accurate.

2. Is it *typical*?

If last week was the only time this year that you spent your allowance on junk food, then her evidence is not typical.

3. Is it *relevant*?

If, in addition, she says you don't deserve a raise because you don't like vegetables, then her evidence is not relevant.

4. Is it *current*?

If she says you spent all your money on junk food two years ago, then her evidence is not current.

5. Is it *adequate*?

If she says you can't have a raise because you spent five cents of your one dollar allowance on junk food, then her evidence is not adequate.

B.   *AUTHORITIES*

1. Is the authority *identified*?

Authorities must be clearly named.

2. Is the authority *professional*?

If the authority does not know anything about farming, then he or she should not be cited as a professional on the subject of farming.

3. Is the authority *current*?

If the issue is farming, and the authority hasn't farmed in twenty years, then even though the person majored in agricultural science in college in 1955, he or she is not a current authority.

4. Is the authority *representative*?

If 86 farmers choose to prune citrus trees annually, and one farmer does not, that farmer is not a representative authority on the annual pruning of citrus trees.

C.   GENERALIZATION

1. Is the generalization based on a sample which is *typical*?

   If the issue is the efficiency of a bicycle, and a sample bicycle is tested which has an extra gear, then that bicycle's efficiency is not typical of bicycles lacking that extra gear.

2. Is the generalization based on a sample which is a *significant percentage of the whole*?

   If one thousand people drive 1967 stick shift Fords, and only one of those people is surveyed, then that sample (.1%) is not a significant percentage of the whole.

3. Is the generalization based on a sample which is *truly representative of the whole*?

   If 13% of the voters are in favor of a proposal, and 87% of the voters are opposed to it, then if only the 13% in favor are quoted, that sample is not truly representative of the whole.

Be on the alert for and question the "too easy" answer. Such an answer usually comes in one of two forms. The first is *the over-simplified cause and effect relationship.* (For example: It rained yesterday and today I have a cold—therefore, the rain gave me a cold. Or, Tom washes his hair every day and always gets good grades—therefore, if I wash my hair every day I will always get good grades.)

The second kind of "too easy" answer comes in the form of *the all or nothing proposition.* (For example: Sally says she wants us to have a school dance, but she didn't come to the third planning meeting—therefore, she really does not want a school dance. Or, either you do your homework and get an A, or you don't do it and fail.)

Second Handout (Day One)

ADVERTISING NEEDS NO APOLOGISTS

The Advertising Council, public service arm of the advertising profession, yesterday staged its first meeting in Los Angeles since it was formed 18 years ago.

Some quasi-intellectuals make it part of their credo to belittle all advertising as a crass and venal huckstering. The answer to them, and it's a clincher, is simply this: try to imagine our way of life without the vital force of advertising in making industry function. We still would be an agricultural economy, tied to the local trading post, if it hadn't been for the development of advertising to promote mass sales. You can have the most sophisticated industrial technology, but if you don't sell industry's products, industry doesn't develop and expand. The countries where advertising has functioned best as a business catalyst are the countries where the standards of living are the highest. In 18 years the Council has sponsored campaigns in behalf of the U.S. Savings Bonds, community charity, polio control, highway safety, mental health, the Red Cross, better schools, aid to higher education and forest fire prevention.

The Council in these campaigns contributed some 170,000,000 dollars in time, talent, and advertising space. It would be hard to support a charge of huckstering in the face of that record. No community in the U.S. but has benefitted from these public service efforts. Recent public opinion surveys show that a preponderant majority of Americans believe advertising is necessary to maintain our standard of living, and is responsible for its present eminence.

This confidence has been earned.

editorial, L.A. Mirror-News Oct. 30, 1959

In addition to the handouts, assemble and bring to class a few samples of the literature of various groups with strong opinions on specific issues [the Sierra Club, the John Birch Society, the American Communist Party, Common Cause].

ACTIVITY   Day One

Tell the class that today marks the beginning of several weeks' work on logic, analysis, and propaganda. Explain that you are going to work together to develop a method to evaluate the reliability of what people say and what people write.

Begin by discussing the nature of proof. You may wish to point out that *logical proof* is made up of three components: evidence [of 1800 homeowners interviewed, 1693 said their property taxes were much too high], authorities [the interviews were done by a professional interviewing organization and the people surveyed were indeed homeowners],

175

and generalizations [most homeowners believe their property taxes are much too high].

Using examples of faulty logic (such as those on the preceding "Tests of Logic" handout), help the class decide on what makes evidence reliable. Based on the class discussion, identify the qualities of reliable evidence. As students identify these qualities, label them, and list them on the chalkboard. Your list should include: accurate, typical, relevant, current, and adequate.

Then, using the same procedure, discuss the nature of reliable authorities. Again, identify and list on the board the four main qualities of reliable authorities: that they be identified, professional, current, and representative.

Again using examples of faulty logic, discuss the nature of reliable generalizations. Identify, label, and list on the board the three main qualities of reliable generalizations: that they be typical, a significant percentage of the whole, and truly representative of the whole.

Now distribute the "Advertising Needs No Apologists" handout and ask the students to read it—looking for any statements which they feel are reliable, whether as evidence, as conclusion derived from an authority, or as a generalization. Explain that you are not asking whether or not they agree with the point of view expressed in the handout, but only for proven statements of fact about advertising.

In the course of determining that few statements of fact are present, ask the class to list a number of questions which they feel must be answered before the facts alleged in the handout can be considered proven, and list these questions on the board. Your list might include such questions as:

1. "Some quasi-intellectuals make it a part of their credo to belittle all advertising . . ." Who are these intellectuals?

2. "We still would be an agricultural economy, tied to the local trading post, if it hadn't been for the development of advertising to promote mass sales." What evidence do we have as proof?

3. "The countries where advertising has functioned best as a business catalyst are the countries where the standards of living are the highest." What proof do we have of this generalization?

In the process of generating these questions, be sure to relate each one of them to one or more of the tests of logic which you have written on the chalkboard. [Authorities must be identified. Evidence must be adequate. Generalizations must be based on a sample which is truly representative of the whole.]

Then ask your students, as homework, to find and bring to the next class one printed statement on any issue or subject which meets at least one of the three tests of logic. That is, they must find a reliable piece of evidence, a statement by a reliable authority on a subject, or a reliable generalization about a subject. Point out that they must be able to successfully apply *all* of the handout tests under the general category of evidence, authorities, or generalizations to the statement they find. [If evidence is accurate but not current, then it cannot be considered logically proven; if an authority is identified and current but not professional, then that person cannot be considered logically trustworthy.] The statement students choose must contain its own logical proof, and not require any further research. They may use magazines, newspapers, or books to locate such a statement. Give them the "Tests of Logic" handout to use as reference.

SPECIAL POINTS   Day One

We do not use the formal terms of logic [*post hoc*, faulty analogy, false dilemma] because we have found that such terms make both logic and argument too academic and too separate from the actual experience of our students.[1]

We give students the handout "Tests of Logic" only after the class has discussed and labelled their own requirements for logical argument. If the students receive the handout at the beginning of the discussion, the quality and intensity of their attention during discussion is diminished. If they receive the handout at the end of their discussion, however, it serves both as a summary of the work they have done in class and as a checklist as they study the literature of their chosen cause at home (see below).

We save the "too easy answer" discussion for Day Two because of the quantity of material which must be covered in Day One.

---

1. If students wish to know more about formal logic, refer them to *Fallacy: The Counterfeit of Argument*, by W. Ward Fearnside and William B. Holther (New Jersey: Prentice-Hall, Inc., 1959).

Handout for Day Two

A CAUSE—ORAL REPORT

This is the first part of a two-part exercise. In this part, you will attempt to identify techniques of propaganda which an interest group uses to support its point of view on an issue.

To begin, pick an interest group which has a strong point of view about an issue which interests you. Then pick a second interest group which has a strong point of view contrary to the first group's point of view (for instance, the Sierra Club vs. Exxon on the question of offshore drilling for oil). Obtain literature from both groups which sets forth their opinions on the issue.

Now pick one of those two groups and plan to interview a spokesperson from that group. In order to prepare for the interview, read the literature from both groups. Using the tests of logic, make a list of all statements made by the group you picked which are unproven. Make another list of statements made by that same group which are contradicted by statements from the second group.

You will be allowed time in class to work with a partner to develop interview questions based on these two lists. You and your partner will also be given time to locate propaganda techniques in the literature (using the handout "Techniques of Propaganda"). When you and your partner have added any other questions about the issue you can think of which were not covered in the literature, hold the interview with the spokesperson. The object of this interview is not to explore the personality of the spokesperson but to see what answers he or she makes to the various questions on your list.

Prior to the interview, you do not need to have already formed your own opinion on the issue, although obviously you may do so. You do need to be able to test the group's logic, and to isolate and identify as many propaganda techniques used by the group as you can.

After you have completed the interview, prepare notes for a 10-minute oral report to the class on the logic of the group's position and on all the propaganda techniques, both written and spoken, which you observed them using. This presentation should not cover your personal views on the issue.

Begin your presentation with a description of your chosen group's

178

point of view on the issue. Then evaluate the logic of that point of view in terms of their evidence, their authorities, and their generalizations. Finally, list as many specific propaganda techniques as you can, each with examples, which are used by the group in its literature and by its spokesperson. Cite direct quotes from the literature and from the interview to support your points.

Be sure that you and your partner divide the actual oral presentation equally between you.

ACTIVITY   Day Two

Begin Day Two by discussing the two items from the "Tests of Logic" handout which were not discussed on Day One: the over-simplified cause and effect relationship, and the all or nothing proposition.

Then have volunteers read to the class the written statements they found for homework, and ask the class to examine the statements one at a time using the "Tests of Logic" handout. This process provides a useful opportunity to review the meaning of each test on the handout.

When several statements have been read and tested in group discussion, and you feel the students understand the "Tests of Logic," distribute the "A Cause—Oral Report" handout. Review the assignment with the class, pointing out that they must choose one issue and two groups with opposing views on that issue. They must use literature from both groups to inform themselves on the issue, and then interview a spokesperson from *one* of the two groups. During that interview they are to seek answers to a list of questions which they have prepared. Remind them that in order to prepare an oral report for the class on the group's logic and use of propaganda, they will need to use the "Tests of Logic" handout and the "Techniques of Propaganda" handout (received in the preceding exercise, "Introduction to Propaganda," page 167).

Explain to the class that a later part of "A Cause" will require them to research the issue further and to take a position on it themselves, but that this part concentrates on just two tasks: first, examining the logic used in the group's literature and by the group's spokesperson; and second, seeking to locate and identify as many techniques of propaganda used by the group as possible.

Show the students the sample interest group literature you have brought to class as examples of the kind of literature you want them to obtain. Then divide the class into pairs and ask each pair to spend some time in discussion in order to pick an issue and two opposing interest groups involved with that issue. Ask each pair to check their selection with you so that you can make sure the interest groups really do disagree on that specific issue. If necessary, allow students a day or two to make a final selection. [Some organizations whose points of view on issues we have found provocative are: General Motors vs. Nader's Raiders, Exxon vs. The Sierra Club, Americans for Democratic Action vs. The John Birch Society.]

Give the students a two week deadline for the oral presentation. Tell them that in class, one week from today, you will discuss interviewing techniques and the kinds of questions they will want to ask their spokespersons. Tell them to be sure to have obtained and analyzed the literature by that time. Also tell the students to bring the handout "Techniques of Propaganda" (from "Introduction to Propaganda," page 167) to the class on Day Three.

SPECIAL POINTS   Day Two

We try to arrange the pairs to avoid personality clashes because the students will be forced to work together intimately for a long period of time.

We divide the class into groups of two so that even though each student analyzes the literature on his own, the partners can develop with each other the questions for the interview. In this way each can use the other as a source of information as well as a sounding board for his own arguments. The partners can also help each other practice analyzing the propaganda techniques to which they have just recently been exposed (in the exercise "Introduction to Propaganda").

If more than one pair of students chooses to analyze the same issue, we encourage them to do so. If several groups research one issue, they can provide a broader spectrum of information about the issue for one another, and for the entire class during the oral presentations.

If, however, more than one pair of students choose to work on the same group's views on the same issue, we discourage them. A group often has only one spokesperson for a particular issue, and in such cases the spokesperson may not be willing to give more than one interview to students from the same class. The interviews need to be conducted by students in pairs rather than in larger groups so that each student has the opportunity to ask some of the prepared questions, and to practice analyzing and questioning, on the spot, the logic of the arguments being presented to him.

For days Two through Four, remind students to bring their "Techniques of Propaganda" and "Tests of Logic" handouts to class. As they prepare their interview questions and, later, as they work on their oral presentations, they should use these handouts to test their own arguments and the arguments of the cause they are investigating.

The process of locating the group, the literature, and the spokesperson for a cause is in itself an enlightening endeavor. The students need to become detectives. Advise them to use the phone book, the library, the newspapers, and to pursue all available leads. Often one organization interested in an issue can help track down another organization interested in the same issue from a different point of view.

ACTIVITY   Day Three   (one week later)

After the student pairs have read the literature of both groups, but before they have done their interviews, review interviewing techniques with the class. You may wish to hand out "Interviews," and, if necessary, run a sample interview in class (see "The Interview," page 150).

Emphasize that the interview should focus on logical argument, not on personalities, and that the interview questions should focus on the group's opinion on the issue, not on the people answering the questions. Have the class as a group develop a number of sample questions which will help the students maintain such a focus. These questions might include: What are the group's sources of information? Who are the experts involved? What are their credentials? Emphasize to the class that their questions should cover the evidence, the authorities who offer the evidence, and the generalizations based on that evidence.

Now have each pair of students make a list of questions (based on their lists of unproven and/or contradicted statements which they prepared as homework). They will ask these questions of the group representative they plan to interview. Allow yourself time in class to review each set of questions with the interviewers to give them support and guidance. Also schedule time for the student pairs to locate propaganda techniques in their group's literature as preparation for the oral report.

Remind the students that before they hold the interview they must decide which of them will record the answers to their questions and which of them will ask them; that only careful notetaking (or taping) will provide the precise information they will need for the rest of the assignment.

SPECIAL POINTS   Day Three

You may wish to take some time with your class to point out some techniques of oral presentation. Remind the students that they should practice their presentation enough times to be confident of what they are saying. They should use notes on notecards, but they should only glance at them—looking at their audience as they speak. Also remind them that a poised speaker is much easier to listen to than one who distracts the audience with nervous gestures.

Handouts for Day Four

A CAUSE—ESSAY

Write a 4–6 page paper on the issue you have been examining, taking and defending a specific point of view about that issue.

To do this, begin by locating two other pieces of written material on the issue. If possible, at least one of these pieces should *not* have been prepared by an interest group. Try an encyclopedia, relevant U.S. Government statistics, or other reference sources or textbooks.

After you have read these new pieces, make up your mind on the issue (if you have not done so already), formulate a thesis statement incorporating your point of view, and write a paper advancing your thesis.

This part of "A Cause" is not concerned with propaganda. Therefore, pay no attention to propaganda used by others and avoid using any propaganda yourself.

Instead, concentrate your paper on logical argument. Offer whatever evidence, authorities, and generalizations you can from your sources which you feel are logically proven to back up your point of view. Be sure to footnote each piece of evidence.

If necessary, you may offer an opinion even though you cannot logically prove your opinion is correct. If you do this, however, you must clearly acknowledge that your point of view is logically unproven. Advance as much evidence and as many authorities and generalizations as you can to justify and explain why you feel the way you do about the issue.

Whether or not you feel your opinion can be logically proven, you must mention and take into account whatever logical evidence, authorities, and generalizations are advanced in opposition to your point of view by the literature (or spokesperson) from the other side(s).

Along with your paper, be sure to hand in whatever pamphlets or other literature you obtained from the various interest groups which you cite in your essay.

Second Handout (Day Four)

OUTLINES

When you have something complicated to write about, making an outline helps you decide what points you want to make and the order in which you want to make them. Outlining will often help your writing style, too. When you have your thoughts arranged on your outline, you can pay much more attention to the way you write about them than you could if you had to unscramble your thoughts while you were writing.

Here is a seven-step way to write an outline:

Step 1: Start by jotting down on a piece of paper every idea that comes to mind about your topic. Don't worry about the order or the relative importance of the ideas; just write them down as they occur to you. This list of ideas will be the source for your outline, so be as complete as you can. You don't have to write up each idea in detail. If you wish, you can simply jot down a few key words or a phrase—whatever is enough to remind you of the idea.

Step 2: When your master list of ideas is as complete as you can make it, go over it and group together ideas which relate to the same point. You can do this by rewriting the list. Or, you can assign a number to each different major point on the list and write the same number next to each idea which relates to that point.

Step 3: When you have grouped all your ideas, look at each group individually. What is the general point to which all the ideas in the group are related? In some cases you will have written out this general point. If you have not, do so at this time.

Step 4: Now look at each general point. How does it relate to the topic you have chosen? If you find several general points which do not relate to your topic, you may want to eliminate them, modify the topic, or modify some of the general points to achieve better unity.

Step 5: When your topic and general points are unified, decide on the order in which you want to write about each general point and number each one accordingly.

Step 6: Now take a new sheet of paper and write down each general point. This time, don't just write a few key words. Instead, write each point out in the form of a sentence which states the point as clearly as possible. You may find one or two of your points hard or even impossible to write out in this way. That means either the point is not appropriate, or it has not been fully thought out. Think it over, and discard that point or rework it.

Step 7: To compose the final outline, take another sheet of paper and write down the sentence describing the first general point. Then write down—again in sentence form—each idea from your original list that relates to this general point. Indent these ideas under the general point in the order you wish to write about them.

You may find that some of these subordinate ideas are more important than others. If so, you may want to indent the less important ones under the more important ones to which they belong:

    I. General Point
       A. Important Subordinate Idea
         1. Minor Subordinate Idea

You may want to number each general point and number or letter each idea under each general point.

ACTIVITY   Day Four   (one week later)

Before you ask the students to begin giving their oral reports (which are due today), distribute "A Cause—Essay." Review the assignment with the class, pointing out that this is their chance to develop as logical a position as possible on their chosen issue—to strip away all the propaganda and fuzzy thinking which they may have encountered.

Explain that you have asked them to locate two additional pieces of literature on the issue so that they will be even more fully informed. If possible, you would like at least one of these pieces of literature *not* to come from an interest group, so students will have one reference which may be more factual and objective than an interest group's literature.

Set a deadline for the paper to be handed in, allowing about two weeks for its completion.

Also distribute and review the handout on outlines, noting that the students will have a great deal of source material with which to work, and that an outline will help them give order to this material.

Allow several days for the students to complete the oral reports. They can be working on their evaluative papers as homework while the oral reports are being given in class.

SPECIAL POINTS   Day Four

We ask students to take a position on the issues which they have researched because it requires them to use the critical tools they have developed in the exercise to evaluate their own thinking and writing. Taking a position helps them to see, as well, that when using such critical tools they must take into account conflict and compromise. Often students come to realize that there can be no perfect solutions to complex problems.

If there is time, in-class workshops during the preparation of this paper can be invaluable, for then the teacher can help with the assessment of the evidence and support students through the process of taking a position on the problem.

By restricting the number of sources, we have found that we can get students to look at the quality of their sources more closely. The argument will thus ride on the quality, rather than the quantity, of the thinking.

SPECIAL POINTS   (General Comments)

This series of activities moves the student out of the classroom and into the community. Students learn how to deal with the logic and language of real issues rather than hypothetical issues posed in an academic setting.

The interview with a spokesperson puts students in an unfamiliar circumstance and requires them to think quickly. They are asked to sift through information and arguments which they cannot predict will be offered, to test the techniques which they have analyzed in class, and to try to evaluate the logic of what is being said.

This exercise is a long one, but it is not as complicated as it may at first appear to be. Each step is carefully delineated and builds on the previous step. We urge you to provide enough time to complete the entire exercise.

Do not use this exercise if the literature and spokespersons for a variety of causes are not easily accessible to your students. If you live in a relatively isolated area and are willing to allow more time for the completion of the exercise, have your students write away for literature and seek out, for the interview, local adherents to the causes they are researching.

THE TWIN PROBLEM—WHAT ACTUALLY HAPPENED[1]

The real-life outcome of The Twin Problem was that the doctor did not operate and Irene died.

The doctor felt that it was morally wrong for anyone to take control of another person's body against that person's will. Although Meg was young, she had enough of a grasp of the issues involved to come to the decision that seemed right to her. The doctor reasoned that if he were to admit the possibility that another person could overrule Meg's decision and force her to undergo a serious and possibly fatal operation, he would uncover an insoluble list of problems: who should have that right? under what circumstances? for what purpose? who should have the right to decide the answers to these questions?

Once they decided not to operate, the doctor and his colleagues did everything they could to protect Meg. They told both her and her parents that Irene was too ill to have a transplantation performed. They said that even if Meg were willing to give her sister one of her kidneys, Irene was so ill that her system would not be able to withstand the shock of the operation.

The doctors tried hard to help the Waterhouses see why Meg was so angry—that she had been neglected by them while they were busily lavishing their love on Irene. After Irene died, the Waterhouses tried to make up for their earlier neglect of Meg. Unfortunately, their efforts met with only partial success, and today Meg is still a highly troubled person.

Note: We first learned this story in the late 1960's. At that time we were told only that the doctors had not operated. Then, in 1977, as part of our final research for this book, we checked back with the distinguished professor who taught The Twin Problem at Harvard, Dr. Lewis Dexter of Boston's Peter Bent Brigham Hospital. Only then did we learn that, in addition to not operating, the doctors had been able to protect Meg from the knowledge of her responsibility in her sister's death. In the period between our first and second encounter with Dr. Dexter, we have taught The Twin Problem to hundreds of students. Yet, although many people thought the doctor should not operate, no one thought up the ancillary idea that Meg should be protected from the knowledge that she could have saved her sister's life.

---

1. This is the solution to "The Twin Problem," page 134.

5 MOTIVATORS

The activities and exercises in this section may be used at any time during a writing course. The section offers ways to help reluctant writers, blocked writers, and self-conscious writers. One exercise encourages writers to weigh the meaning of words. The last two exercises encourage students to play with words.

SILENT CLASS

PURPOSE AND DESCRIPTION

A classroom activity which demonstrates the communicative power of the written word. Useful with beginning students who are reluctant or uncertain writers. All communication in the class is restricted to words written on the chalkboard.

LEVEL   Beginning.

CLASS PERIODS   One.

ADVANCE PREPARATION   None.

ACTIVITY

At the start of the class, wait until all talking has stopped, go to the chalkboard, write "silence is golden" (without quotes) on it, hand the chalk to one of the students, and sit in one of the student chairs. The students will soon catch on that this is a new game with very simple rules: 1) no talking, and 2) the person who has the chalk may write on the board and then must hand the chalk over to another student. Of course you may stop the exercise at any time, but it is most effective if you let it run for the entire classroom period.

SPECIAL POINTS

This activity brings out nearly all of the most reluctant writers because they find that they must write in order to communicate anything at all.

If you have a class that is hard to control, we suggest you avoid this exercise, as a few unruly students can quickly spoil it.

This is a conversation of the class with itself, and the topics will be as diverse as the students themselves. There will be pauses, repetitions, and boring spots, just as there are in ordinary spoken conversations. The key to success is to allow the process to continue without intervening (except as noted below). When the students see that the responsibility for an interesting exchange rests entirely with them, they will behave as they would in a spoken exchange and lead the writing into areas which interest them.

The exercise is most fun when there is no spoken conversation at all. You can help this happen by not speaking yourself from the opening of class to the closing bell. Reply to questions at the beginning of class by pressing a finger to your lips, and students will quickly gather that something unusual is going on.

Choose the first student you give the chalk to carefully. Pick one who is not self-conscious, so he or she will not mind standing up in front of the class, and one who is adventuresome, so the "conversation" will get off to an interesting start.

The one time when we suggest you intervene is if you spot a written move toward pettiness or personal comment, as this is one avenue which will cause the exercise to deteriorate swiftly. If you see the "conversation" taking such a turn, take the chalk when the student is finished and write whatever seems appropriate on the board to get things back on the track.

We advise the omission of quotation marks from "silence is golden" as their inclusion is likely to precipitate a stream of aphorisms and discourage the kind of conversation desired.

When and how much to erase once the board starts to get full may cause quite a bit of written discussion. Don't be afraid to stay out of the debate—the students will work it out for themselves.

ONE WORD AT A TIME

PURPOSE AND DESCRIPTION

A classroom activity to encourage students to play with words and weigh their meanings. Students have a written dialogue with one another during which they are allowed to exchange only one word at a time.

LEVEL   Beginning.

CLASS PERIODS   One.

ADVANCE PREPARATION   None.

ACTIVITY

Ask the students to seat themselves in pairs so that each has a partner he does not know well. Tell the students that they are going to have a written conversation with their partner, but that in this conversation they can use only one word at a time.

To begin, ask each student to write one word at the top of a piece of paper. Along with this single word, they may also use punctuation, but they may not use any gestures or looks. After these single words are written, ask the partners to exchange papers. Each student will now have a word to respond to and the task of selecting the one word with which he wants to respond.

When all the students have responded, have the partners exchange papers. In this way every pair is working on two separate conversations, each on a separate piece of paper. The exchanges may take place as many times as the students can remain focused on the activity. There should be at least eight exchanges.

When the partners are finished writing, have each one read carefully to himself the list of words on one of the two papers to which he contributed. Now ask the students if any of their lists of words clearly make sense as conversation. If some say *yes*, ask one of those students to read that conversation out loud to the class. After the words are read, have a second class member who was not involved in that conversation paraphrase the conversation or elaborate on it. Then ask the student

193

who read the conversation out loud if the other student's understanding of it jibes with his own. If not, where was the meaning lost or misinterpreted? Why? Did a word get used ambiguously or in a misleading way? Were the partners responding to the most recent developments in the conversations or to preconceptions about where they wanted the conversations to go?

In follow-up discussion, you may want to have the partners read out loud both conversations they had with one another. Then ask the other students to compare the subjects, tones, and degrees of communication of these conversations.

After a number of conversations have been shared and discussed, encourage all the students to re-read the conversations they worked on, to consider the many possible meanings for each word written, and to look for any flow or momentum their conversations may have acquired.

If students find that some of their conversations entirely lack continuity, consider with the whole group why these particular exchanges missed each other.

SPECIAL POINTS

Since people depend heavily on context and gesture to give meaning to their words, they often choose words casually with little conscious effort. This exercise, in contrast, requires each student to give his utmost attention to every word he uses, to weigh and determine its denotations, connotations, and implications.

Our students say that one reason they enjoy this activity is that it gives them an easy way to make a little contact with classmates who might otherwise remain beyond reach. Our main reason, though, for having these conversations take place between students who do not know one another well is that we want their exchanges to depend more purely on word impact than on a shared personal knowledge of one another.

This activity gives a good indication of which students can play with words and which students feel intimidated by them. The latter tend to rule out shades of meaning and stick closely to literal or limited interpretations only.

FREE FLOW

PURPOSE AND DESCRIPTION

To help students use the technique of free association to locate a source of productive personal topics and rich detail. Students free associate at home, and then in class examine their material for topic ideas and detail.

LEVEL   Any.

CLASS PERIODS   One-third plus one.

ADVANCE PREPARATION   None.

ACTIVITY   Day One

Near the end of a class period tell your students that for homework they are to set aside 45 undisturbed minutes in which to record the flow of their thoughts. Tell them that in the "free flow" of their thoughts is a reservoir of ideas as well as a rich source of graphic detail, and that you will show them how to retrieve this material after they have written their own "free flow." Stress that a quiet atmosphere and relative seclusion are important, and that if this is impossible to find at home, a park or library may be better. Tell them that in this secluded place they are to free associate, jotting down every word or idea that comes to mind. Point out that there is no right or wrong way to do this, that only following and recording their freely flowing thought-stream is important. If nothing comes to mind, tell them to repeatedly write the word "nothing" until a new thought comes. At the end of the 45 minutes they are to stop. Have them bring their associations to class the following day.

Day Two

Begin the day's activity by discussing the usual method your students use to find essay topics. [Do they think of one subject in a number of different ways? Do they think of details and create a topic to cover most of the details? Do they have a predominant feeling which seems to color everything they think about? Or do they, as do our students, often find they have "nothing" to write about?] Now, in your discussion explain

195

that you are going to show them a way in which they themselves may always be the best source of their material by using their own free associations. Ask them to read over their associations—looking for repeated themes or images, engaging sounds or phrases which can point the way toward productive topics.

As your students work on their associations, move through the class helping those who may have gotten stuck. Occasionally, we have found our students unable to find topics from their associations because they have associated in rather narrow ways [car, Dodge, Chevrolet, Ford; or house, bedroom, living room, dining room, kitchen]. You will need to help these students enrich their list of associations by asking them why they think they made their choices. [What attracted them to certain categories? Did they report on what they were looking at? Did they edit out certain ideas which came to mind?] The answers to such questions will encourage them back into the associative process.

After each student has located a topic, have the students reread their associations—listing details from them which support that topic. The list of details may include single words or phrases, anecdotes, or images. Have students look for strings of details which often follow a relatively abstract idea. Many times, these are just the details papers need for vividness. Point out to the class that, while they are making the list of details, new associations may occur to them. These, too, should be included in the lists. Now have each student repeat the whole process of finding a new essay topic and its supporting detail. Some of the details used to support the first topic may also be used for the second.

At the end of the period, have your students hand in their topic and detail lists along with their associations. Tell the class that using free association to find topics and detail works even better in an entirely private situation—when they themselves will be the only ones to see the associations.

SPECIAL POINTS

This exercise is particularly effective at the beginning of the year when students most need to believe in and articulate their storehouse of topics. It moves them, again and again, back upon themselves, and they find that they do, indeed, have something to say.

Make sure, also, that your students understand that if they free associate in a place where they can be easily distracted, both the personal nature of their associations and the quality of their detail will be diminished.

Assure your students that they may edit their associations before they hand them in, if they feel there is something they wish not to share with you, but that in any case the associations will always be kept confidential.

CONCENTRATING

PURPOSE AND DESCRIPTION

A classroom activity which demonstrates an effective way to become less self-conscious and awkward in writing.

LEVEL   Any.

CLASS PERIODS   One or less.

ADVANCE PREPARATION   None.

ACTIVITY

This is one of the more unusual activities in this book and we urge you to try it if your students are self-conscious about their writing. It is easy for a teacher to say "concentrate on your subject," but almost impossible for students to really understand this abstract advice. This activity *shows* students, through the concrete evidence of their own bodies, the power of their concentration.

Divide the class into two parts. Explain that they are going to participate in an unusual exercise, the purpose of which will become clear to them at the conclusion of the exercise. Sit among the students and remain seated among them as much as possible during the exercise. Have the first half of the class stand in a line facing the seated second half. Tell the standing students to simply stand quietly. Tell the seated students to look carefully and closely at the standing students and to notice everything about them. The standing students will soon become quite self-conscious and ill at ease as a result of being stared at by their comfortably seated classmates. Then have the two halves change places. The new standing group will also become uncomfortable.

Then have the first half stand again in front of the seated second half. This time give the standing group something clearly visible to count while the seated students again watch them. It may be acoustical tiles, cinderblocks in the walls, or linoleum squares on the floor. Tell them to concentrate hard on counting and recounting out loud. This time they will lose their self-consciousness and think about the counting. Then have the two halves change places for the last time. The second group should also count, and will also lose self-consciousness.

Once all are reseated, ask the students to compare how they felt the first time they stood in front of their classmates with how they felt the second time. Get them to talk about their bodies—how they stood, what they did with their hands. It will quickly become clear to the students that the first time they were self-conscious, and the second time they were not.

Help the students determine that what saved them from self-consciousness the second time was their concentration on the activity you asked them to perform. Most will say that their bodies felt awkward when they were simply being stared at; but once they had something to take their minds off the fact that they were being watched, they forgot entirely about their bodies and felt at ease.

Then tell the students that the relevance of this exercise for a writing class is the need for a writer to keep his mind firmly on the writing task before him. If he does that, the words will arrange themselves quite well—almost of their own accord—just as the students who had a counting job to do stood gracefully and unself-consciously. When the writer forgets about his subject, and thinks only of his writing style, the flow of words will dry up and he will become hopelessly enmeshed in tortured syntax—just as the students with nothing to do but be aware of themselves being looked at quickly felt awkward and became awkward.

SPECIAL POINTS

This experience creates a touchstone to which you can refer throughout the rest of the course. By experiencing the liberating power of their own focused concentration, students can begin to understand how important and useful it is to make what they are trying to say their primary concern. Many students, paralyzed by general awareness of their grammatical inadequacies or by lack of self-confidence, are unable to write anything at all. For such students, this experience can be a way to help them write more easily and freely. Once they do so, you can help them overcome whatever grammatical difficulties they may have.

Remember that the key to this exercise is concentration. This concentration can only be achieved by the students if you keep the tone of the exercise serious. Keep alert to what both halves of the class are doing during the exercise. During the first part, when the standing students have nothing to do, encourage both groups to really look at one another. During the second part, make sure the standing students are really concentrating on counting. Having them count out loud will help focus their attention.

The seated students will not be self-conscious because you are seated with them, staring with them at the others, and because of psychological factors affecting seated people versus standing people (cf. *The Naked Ape* by Desmond Morris, and *Body Language* by Julius Fast). The seated students become the "audience," and the standing students become the "actors."[1]

---

1. This exercise was derived from *Improvisation for the Theater* by Viola Spolin (Evanston, Illinois: Northwestern University Press, 1963). The book is written for teachers of acting but has many fascinating parallels to the teaching of writing.

FICTIONARY

PURPOSE AND DESCRIPTION

A classroom game which helps develop control of tone, conciseness of style, and dictionary skills. Students write imaginary dictionary definitions for a word and try to pick the real definition from among the fictional ones.

LEVEL   Any.

CLASS PERIODS   One.

ADVANCE PREPARATION

Bring enough dictionaries to class to allow one per 10 students.

ACTIVITY

Write a word and its dictionary definition on the chalkboard. Review with the students the components of such definitions [part of speech, origin, alternative meanings] and discuss the extremely compressed style in which they are written.

Then tell the class that they are going to play a game which involves making up definitions which sound real and trying to identify the real definitions from among made-up ones.

Begin the game by asking one class member to look through the dictionary until he has located a word he does not know. He reads and spells the word—but not the dictionary definition—to the entire class. If no one knows its meaning (students are on their honor to be honest), each student then makes up and writes out an imaginary definition of the word, including its part of speech. The student holding the dictionary writes down the correct dictionary definition, using only the first major definition listed. All the definitions—real and imaginary—are mixed, and the student who knows the correct definition reads them one by one to the class. Then he re-reads them and each student (except for the dictionary holder) votes by raising his hand for the definition he thinks is correct. After all selections are made, the proper definition is revealed, and you score the players as follows:

1 point to the person who chose the word to be defined (the dictionary holder) for each wrong definition selected by another player,

2 points to a player for each time his made-up description was selected by another player as being correct,

3 points to a player who selected the correct definition (except the dictionary holder, of course),

4 points to anyone who can correctly define a word when it is first proposed to the group by the dictionary holder.

The dictionary is then passed to another student who picks a new word, and the game continues.

Have each creator of an imaginary definition write his or her name in the corner so the reader can check vagaries of handwriting and pronunciation with the proper author. The reader should read each definition to himself ahead of time so his presentation will be a smooth one.

Many definitions will be funny. Impress on each reader the obligation to keep a straight face so he will not prejudice classmates' chances.

Have students use pencils to write with and use identical pieces of paper to write on. In that way, when the dictionary holder reads all the definitions to the class, there will be no visual clues to the identity of any author.

SPECIAL POINTS

In addition to being an interesting exercise in tone, Fictionary encourages students to analyze words in terms of roots, prefixes, and suffixes. These elements prove effective in the creation of believable definitions, and sometimes help players select the correct definition.

Ten seems to us to be the maximum number of people who can enjoy this game as a group. We suggest that you divide classes over this size into smaller groups, each with its own dictionary.

You may wish to point out that students holding the dictionary will have a better chance of fooling their classmates if they select a word with a definition which is not highly technical or scientific.

We ask for only one definition of a word. It is too hard for students to maintain control of tone through more than one definition. The reader also reads only the first definition given in the dictionary.

The scoring system encourages students to pick words with definitions which are not obvious and to try to create imaginary definitions which are convincing. Sometimes students will write a silly definition just to get a laugh. Encourage these students to aim for points rather than laughs.

If you feel your class needs a good deal of direction, you may wish to choose the first word yourself to set an example for the students to follow.

SINGLE/DOUBLE/TRIPLE GHOST

PURPOSE AND DESCRIPTION

To give students the experience of playing with words. A classroom game offering players practice in spelling and vocabulary.

LEVEL

Single for beginners, double for intermediates, and triple for advanced.

CLASS PERIODS   One.

ADVANCE PREPARATION

Make sure a good dictionary is available in the classroom.

ACTIVITY

Determine a fixed order of play for each student to follow. The first student picks a letter at random. Each subsequent student adds one letter. A student who intentionally or unintentionally adds a letter to the letter group so that the letters spell a complete word loses the round. Scoring can be adapted to class size: the larger the class, the fewer losses permitted before a student is out of the game.

There are three versions of the game of Ghost. In *Single Ghost*, the first letter chosen must be the start of a word, and each additional letter must be added to the right of the original letter [L, LI, LIN, LINE].

In *Double Ghost*, new letters can be added before as well as after the original letter [N, NE, INE, INES, LINES]. As in Single Ghost, each letter group is supposed to form a part of a legitimate word. However, in Double Ghost it is proper to be thinking of a word which requires additional letters *before* the letter group as well as after it.

In *Triple Ghost*, new letters can be inserted in the middle of the letter group as well as before and after [E, IE, INE, INES, LINES]. In Triple Ghost it is a good idea to make a rule that each letter group in itself be consecutive letters in an acceptable word without requiring the insertion of additional letters in the middle of the letter group. [Player 1: T, perhaps for Tower. Player 2: TT, perhaps for raTTle. Player 3 may *not* say TTT for TaTTle because a letter –A– must be inserted in the middle of the letter group. The letters TTT are not a letter group in a real word.] We suggest you retain this rule except when working with especially gifted students.

In all three versions of the game, if a student wishes, when it is his turn he can challenge the player who added the last letter. If the challenged student can specify a word which derives from the current letter group, the challenger loses. If the challenged student cannot supply a word, the challenger wins. Each student is supposed to have a legitimate word in mind as he adds a letter. However, it is considered fair to add a letter without a word in mind and to hope that the next player will not challenge the addition.

To keep arguments to a minimum, specify that no proper nouns are acceptable, and that the classroom's dictionary is the final arbiter of a word's legitimacy and spelling.

SPECIAL POINTS

We find this game helps students think of words in new ways—as tools, toys, and objects to be manipulated. This helps loosen up students who feel constricted when dealing with words. Often a student gains a feeling of power over words.

You may want to let your students write down the letters as the game progresses, particularly if you are playing Triple Ghost. Some students need to see letters, rather than just hear them, in order to fully appreciate the possible variations.

APPENDICES

SIX COURSE OUTLINES

The course outlines in this section represent only a few of the many ways in which the exercises in this book can be organized. We have allowed time for the use of rhetoric and grammar books in addition to these exercises. Even so, you may find the outlines call for more class time than you have available. Do not hesitate to prune them.

You will notice that some exercises are used in all six outlines. That is because they can be adapted to a variety of levels.

When we plan a course, we know we will modify our outline throughout the course as we learn about our class's particular strengths, weaknesses, and predilections. It is just because of this continual modification process that we organized the Table of Contents in this book by area rather than by level. Nonetheless, these outlines may provide you with useful places from which to begin.

BEGINNING STUDENTS

We assume that our beginning students have had little, if any, work in observation and description; that they need to learn such basic organizational techniques as topic sentences, thesis statements, paragraphing, introductions and conclusions; that they need to learn about word choice, variation of style and revision; that they need exposure to simple research techniques and practice in simple analysis and argument. We also believe that it is of great importance for every beginning student to develop confidence in his ability to write.

BEGINNING STUDENTS–16 WEEKS

Weeks 1–3 Observation

3	First Day Back
215	Corrective Marks
7	The Abstraction Game
34	The Orange
24	Characters
29	A Place in School
21	Childhood Photos

Weeks 4–6 Organization

77	Pictures With a Point
73	Paragraphs in a Circle (repeat once)
101	Terrific Topic Sentences
60	Collective Questioning *or* 66 Portrait
51	Introductions and Conclusions

BEGINNING STUDENTS—32 WEEKS

INTERMEDIATE STUDENTS

We assume that our intermediate students have had some practice in basic descriptive techniques; that they may have been exposed to the concepts of topic sentences and thesis statements; and that they have some understanding of how to organize short essays. We assume that they need to develop further organizational skills and an awareness of style. We also assume that, at best, intermediate students have learned how to write only a very simple research paper and they they have had very limited experience with analysis and argument.

INTERMEDIATE STUDENTS–16 WEEKS

INTERMEDIATE STUDENTS—32 WEEKS

Weeks 18–22 Analysis and Argument

144   From the Newspaper
(all 5 exercises)

140   School

Weeks 23–25 Propaganda

167   Introduction to Propaganda

172   A Cause

Week 26 More Analysis and Argument

134   The Twin Problem

Weeks 27–30 Research Paper

Assigned topic *or* students'
own choice (see On Teaching
Research Papers, page 131)

Weeks 31–32 Final Paper

89   Thesis Times Three

ADVANCED STUDENTS

We assume our advanced students are generally familiar with the narrative, descriptive, and expository essay forms; that they view thesis statements and topic sentences as familiar concepts; and that they are beginning to evolve a personal writing style. We therefore move them fairly quickly through exercises involving fundamental techniques to assignments which ask them to write quite long and complex essays.

ADVANCED STUDENTS—16 WEEKS

Weeks 1–3 Observation

3   First Day Back

215   Corrective Marks

7   The Abstraction Game

26   Quick Study

14   Elementary, My Dear Watson *or*
21 Childhood Photos

37   The Egg

31   High Tension

Weeks 4–5 Organization

51   Introductions and Conclusions

73   Paragraphs in a Circle

85   Place to Place *or* 68 One of the
Family

**Weeks 6–8   Alternative A
Style**

95   Sentence Patterns

117   People Landscapes

126   The Language of Television

119   Audiences

117   People Landscapes

126   The Language of Television

119   Audiences

**Weeks 6–8 Alternative B
Research**

Assigned topic for research
(see On Teaching Research
Papers, page 131)

95   Sentence Patterns

**Weeks 6–8 Alternative C
Analysis**

140   School

95   Sentence Patterns

213

ADVANCED STUDENTS—32 WEEKS

CORRECTIVE MARKS

PURPOSE AND DESCRIPTION

We used to assume that all our students understood the marks we used in correcting their papers, but over the years we discovered that quite a few don't understand them. So, at the beginning of each semester we distribute a list of the marks we use.

LEVEL   Any.

CLASS PERIODS   One-half.

ADVANCE PREPARATION

Duplicate a list of the marks you use when correcting papers. Here is the list we pass out:

Handout

CORRECTIVE MARKS

In the Margin	In the Text	
	~~out~~ *e*	omit crossed out material
	in ∧	insert
tr	t(e\h)	transpose letters as indicated
tr	then ⌠now⌡	transpose words as indicated
sp	(circled)	spelling error
u.c.	the (underlined)	should be a capital letter
l.c.	⁄The	should be a lower case (small) letter
run-on	underlined	a run-on sentence
n.s.	underlined	not a sentence: lacks subject and/or verb

In the Margin	In the Text	
ref	(circled)	faulty pronoun reference
gr	<u>underline</u>	grammar error
awk	<u>underline</u>	phrasing awkward
p	(:)	colon needed here
p	(,)	comma needed here
p	(;)	semicolon needed here
p	(.)	period needed here
	¶	start a new paragraph
	no ¶	do not start a new paragraph
	abc conn ef	what is the connection?
?	<u>underline</u>	meaning unclear
#	(circled)	an unnecessarily abstruse word or phrase used
	[the]	material enclosed in brackets is grammatically correct but may be omitted without loss of meaning

---

ACTIVITY   Distribute and discuss the list.

SPECIAL POINTS

The last four marks are not found in ordinary lists of proofreader's marks. We use the Y conn when the logic is not apparent, the ? when we don't understand, the $ when the writer tries unsuccessfully to sound elegant or sophisticated, and the [ ] when the student is verbose. The distinction between material bracketed and material deleted is sometimes hard for a student to grasp at first. Material bracketed is unnecessary although grammatically correct, while material deleted must be omitted because it is grammatically incorrect.

216

INDEX OF EXERCISES BY WRITING SKILL